W9-BYA-932

Naval Warrior
The Life of
Commodore Isaac Mayo

Attributed to Benjamin West   Maryland State Archives

ISAAC MAYO-1838

Naval
Warrior
The Life of
Commodore
Isaac Mayo

By
Byron A. Lee

"In arms intrepid with the first
he fought,
Fac'd every foe and every
danger sought."
Lines from Homer

Ann Arrundell County Historical Society
Linthicum, Maryland
2002

Naval Warrior
The Life of Commodore Isaac Mayo

Copyright © 2002 Byron A. Lee
All rights reserved. No part of this book may be
reproduced or utilized in any form or by any means,
electronic or mechanical, including photocopying and
recording, or by any information storage and retrieval
system, without permission in writing from the author.

Published by
Ann Arrundell County Historical Society
Linthicum, Maryland 21090-0385

Publisher's Cataloging-in-Publication
Lee, Byron A.
    Naval warrior : the life of Commodore Isaac Mayo / by
Byron A. Lee. -- 1st ed.
    p. cm
    Includes bibliographical references and index.
    ISBN 9702355-1-8
    1. Mayo, Isaac, 1791-1861. 2. Sailors--United States
--Biography. 3. United States. Navy--Biography.
4. United States--History, Naval--To 1900. I. Title.

E182.M44L44 2002   359'.0092
                                    QBI02-200388

Printed in the United States of America
Printed by A&M Printing, Inc., Glen Burnie, MD
Third Printing.

To the memory of
Jack Kelbaugh
and his boundless love of
Anne Arundel County,
its history and heritage

Contents

**SILVER MEDAL AWARDED BY U. S. CONGRESS
TO LIEUTENANT ISAAC MAYO**

Illustrations

Foreword

For the United States as a nation it is useful in understanding the present to have a knowledge of where we came from. That is particularly true in the case of the Navy, a longstanding organization that places great value on tradition. Practices change over time because of advances in technology, social pressures, international concerns, and other considerations. But the Navy's underlying values remain constant. Among them are the concepts of leadership, patriotism, honor, courage, and commitment--as important now as they were in the environment that Commodore Isaac Mayo inhabited in the 19th century. Indeed, as Captain Lee tells us in the fine, well-researched biography that follows, Mayo's final act as a naval officer involved a matter of honor. He offered his resignation from the Navy that he had served so well because he wanted to remain loyal to his home state of Maryland at a time when the Union was being split in two.

As his life unfolds on these pages, Mayo moves through increasingly senior positions of rank and responsibility. He was involved in a great deal of the U.S. Navy's action during his many years of service--twenty-five years of sea duty spread over a period of a half century. He fought in the War of 1812, in which the fledgling United States fought for respect against the powerful Royal Navy of Great Britain. He deployed to the Mediterranean far in advance of our current-day Sixth Fleet.

He was involved in operations in the West Indies, South America, Florida, and Africa, demonstrating the great mobility that is among the assets of the United States Navy. He exhibited his physical courage in the Mexican War when he went ashore to command naval gunfire. The culmination of his career was as commodore on board the frigate *Constitution*, which even today is a commissioned ship of the Navy, an icon to celebrate the service's history. His legacy might have been much brighter (and better known) today if his request had been granted to accompany his contemporary, Commodore Matthew C. Perry, on the opening of Japan by the West in the early 1850s. Such are the vagaries of fortune and opportunity. As it was, he had a full career and did much for his country.

In addition to the value of this book in illuminating the life of a naval officer with an interesting and varied career, it tells us by implication of how very much many aspects of life in the Navy have changed over the course of nearly two centuries. Back then when honor was at stake, for instance, one defended his convictions by risking his life. Isaac Mayo twice challenged his half sister's fiancé to duels because he did not believe the man suitable for her. Now, at a time when the Navy has a strong commitment to equal opportunity, we are reminded that the service's role in racial issues in the mid-19th century was far more basic. It operated warships off the coast of Africa to try to thwart the shipment of slaves; the irony is that Mayo hated slave traders and did his duty on these patrols even though he owned slaves himself.

We read here of a Navy in which flogging was a standard means of enforcing discipline; a time when ships' crews received prize money for successful exploits; naval careers that were essentially intermittent rather than being of continuous service; warships that were armed with muzzle-loading cannon and powered by the wind upon their great canvas sails; and landing parties of sailors who functioned as members of the Marine Corps do to-day. The total number of men in the Navy and Marine Corps of 1835 would be just about the right number to fill out the crew and air wing of a current aircraft carrier. In Mayo's day ships' crews included men who were often foreign born and not by any means all volunteers. They spent long periods away from home with little chance for recreation ashore. Life aboard ship meant relatively primitive food and medical care. It was a hard life that called upon officers such as Mayo to provide the requisite leadership.

As we contemplate the United States Navy of the twenty-first century, with its nuclear-powered warships, mixed-gender crews, jet aircraft, helicopters, complex shore establishment, computer networks, sophisticated electronic sensors, satellite navigation, and worldwide reach, it is well to remember that we got where we are through an evolutionary process shaped at every turn by dedicated human beings. Commodore Isaac Mayo was one of those many humans. His life, with its application of unchanging principles, shows us how much one person can accomplish.

Paul Stillwell
Director, History Division
U.S. Naval Institute
Annapolis, Maryland

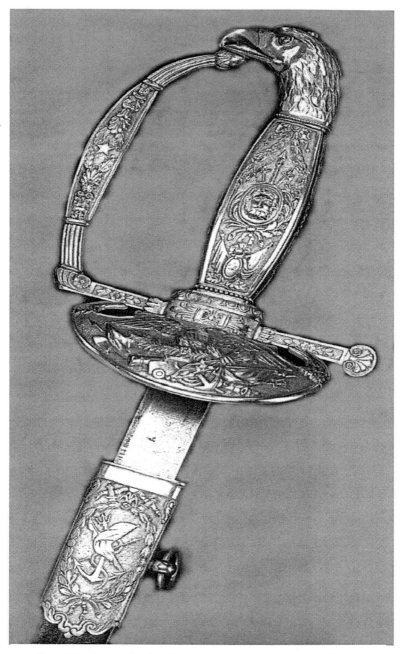

**WAR OF 1812 GOLD EAGLE SWORD
PRESENTED BY STATE OF MARYLAND
TO LIEUTENANT ISAAC MAYO**

Preface

Commodore Isaac Mayo is an almost forgotten United States naval officer from the period between the Revolutionary War and the Civil War. He is not alone among the lost Commodores; however, the area of Maryland south of Annapolis, between the South and Rhode Rivers, is named Mayo after him, and that fact periodically stimulates interest in the source of the name. Over the past 50 years, local newspaper stories, magazine articles, school projects and even a play performed in the Mayo area have touched on his life. This book is the first to explore thoroughly Isaac Mayo's personal life and career.

Even the date of his birth, the nature of his death and the final burial location are uncertain. It is certain that he was a prominent Maryland citizen from Anne Arundel County; that he amassed an estate of more than 1400 acres around his home, Gresham; and that he served in the United States Navy from 1809 to 1861. He had a solid combat record punctuated by long periods of leave which he devoted to his family and his estate. His military record during the War of 1812 was among the finest of his generation. He also saw combat in the Second Seminole War in Florida (1839-1840), in Africa while protecting American interests (1843) and in the Mexican War (1847). His final tour as Commodore was in the *USS Constitution*, a glorious experience in his documented view.

Mayo's service record can be compared with that of

Commodore Matthew Calbraith Perry, the leader of the "Opening of Japan" expedition. These two officers were contemporaries and served together several times. Perry had little combat experience and much shore duty; yet, he became known as "one of the preeminent officers of the antebellum navy" according to his latest biographer.[1] Possible reasons for this disparity in historical perspective, and the reasons for Perry's renown and Mayo's obscurity in history, are explored in this book.

A significant amount of research about Mayo's family and land holdings has been included in the appendices because such information illuminates the nature of his character, personality, and probable motives as he progressed through his naval career. He was a Southerner by birth, inheritance and location of his home, yet he owned only about 10-15 adult slaves for household and transportation assistance. All his land holdings were tilled by tenant farmers. As an Anne Arundel County native, he considered Annapolis the center of the universe; this mindset, along with a well-earned reputation, enabled him to influence the decision to locate the U.S. Naval Academy there in 1845.

Very little documentation has survived from Isaac Mayo's life and career. There are only two journals and a letter book of Mayo papers; most information that exists about his military career is from his official correspondence to the Secretary of the Navy. Such a lack of information often influences would-be biographers and may explain the paucity of attention given to him. It is hoped that this book will stimulate scholarly research on other Maryland naval officers from the antebellum period. There are many interesting, untold stories waiting for the industrious historian.

Acknowledgments

The idea of researching and writing about Commodore Mayo came from the late Mr. Jack Kelbaugh. He enthusiastically provided information that he had gathered over the years, suggested research areas, read some of the early drafts and provided his support for the effort. The book has been dedicated to his memory as a small token of my regard for him.

I received assistance from a number of institutions that I want to acknowledge. Two libraries provided the preponderance of books and microfilm for research on Isaac Mayo: the United States Naval Academy Chester Nimitz Library and the Maryland Hall of Records in Annapolis. Other libraries that contained valuable information were the libraries of the Naval Historical Center in Washington, D.C. and of the Maryland Historical Society in Baltimore, MD. The Mariners' Museum in Newport News, VA, the Navy Museum, the Beverley R. Robinson Collection at the Naval Academy and the Naval Academy Museum were able to locate some rare photographs of former Mayo ship commands and battles. The Ann Arrundell County Historical Society has supported my efforts throughout research and publishing, for which I am especially grateful.

Many individuals have aided in the preparation and publishing of this book. Mark Schatz of the Ann Arrundell County Historical Society acted as my editor. Fred Fetrow, Professor, in the English Department, U.S. Naval Academy, was the editorial assistant. Both read the entire book and made many helpful suggestions. Paul Stillwell, U.S. Naval Institute, wrote the Foreword pointing out that the underlying values of the Navy today and in Mayo's era are constant. James Cheevers of the Naval Academy Museum was particularly helpful in obtaining photographs and in the research on the Naval Academy Cemetery and the origins of the Naval Academy. Sigrid Trumpy and Leah Hubicsak of the Beverley R. Robinson Collection helped with photographs of prints in their collection. Jean Hort, Director, Navy Department Library, helped with the Isaac Mayo Journals and letter book. William J. Pierson photographed sites, artifacts and photographs for use in the book. Delegate Virginia Clagett helped obtain the photograph of the painting of Commodore Mayo from the State Archives. Leon Johnson and his wife provided a photograph of their home, Gresham. Owen Daly provided enthusiastic support from the Mayo family descendants. Tom Bailliere made Commodore Mayo's artifacts in his possession available for inspection and photographing. Rosemary Dodd reviewed the Mayo genealogy appendix. Janice E. Wilson typed portions of the book that were published in the *Anne Arundel County History Notes*. Finally, my wife, Donna, played an invaluable role by encouraging and supporting the considerable effort to research and write this book

It has been my privilege to have lived, for the past three years, with the surviving records and artifacts from the career of a brave and devoted naval officer, Isaac Mayo.

1
Isaac Mayo's
Personal Life

*"If it is a crime to be possessed of ample
wealth and move about like a Gentleman....
I plead guilty to the charges."*
Isaac Mayo, 1854

Isaac Mayo had two principal interests during his life, the U.S. Navy and his estate which became known as "Gresham." His property was located in Anne Arundel County between the South and Rhode Rivers on the western shore of the Chesapeake Bay, about five miles south of Annapolis, Maryland, in an area now called Mayo. His great-grandfather, Joshua Mayo, first appeared in the area records in 1707 when he married Hannah Learson in the All Hallows Parish, Md.[1] Isaac Mayo wrote in his journal that Joshua immigrated from Wales.[2] Joshua's oldest, and only surviving son, was Joseph Mayo, Isaac Mayo's grandfather. Joseph married twice with fourteen children total from both families; Isaac's father, Isaac, Sr., was the oldest son in the second family.

Joseph became a successful plantation owner and accumulated a considerable amount of land. He also was a strong backer of the American Revolution. Isaac, Jr. would later write that Charles Carroll, signer of the Declaration of Independence, said of his grandfather, " He is one of the most uncompromising (supporters) of the revolution; he would hear of nothing short of downright independence."[3] When Joseph died he willed land to all of his sons in his second family. Isaac, Sr. received 300 acres in two parcels called "Collersly" and "Brewer's Chance." His son, Samuel, was to receive one half of "Selby's Marsh" (250 acres), which Joseph bought from John Gresham in 1765, provided that Samuel lived to the age of 21 years.[4]

The property, Selby's Marsh, contained a house called Gresham, which had been owned by several generations of John Greshams. How this property became the cornerstone of Isaac Mayo's estate is somewhat convoluted. Joseph Mayo's will states that if Samuel dies before he is 21, the property is to go to Isaac, Sr. Samuel did live and inherited the land, but died in 1801; however Isaac, Sr. had died in 1797.[5] Samuel left Selby's Marsh to Isaac, Jr. when he became 18 years of age provided he gave up his claim to the the parcel of 150 acres called Collersly that Isaac, Sr. had left in his will to Isaac, Jr.[6] Isaac, Jr. did choose the Selby Marsh land which contained the Gresham house. Gresham is described in the 1798 Federal Direct Tax rolls as a 30 ft. x 16 ft. one-story house, far smaller than the imposing structure now on the site.

The date of the birth of Isaac Mayo, Jr. is inconsistently listed in various places. His obituary cited his birthdate as Sept. 19, 1791, and the census for 1860 stated that he was of the age that would place his birth in 1791. The 1850 census would indicate that he was born in 1793, while the Naval Academy Cemetery monument lists him as having been born in 1795. Most authors have used 1795 as his birth year. The 1790 census and the wills of Samuel and Isaac, Sr. give some

clues that suggest he was born before 1795. The census indicates that Isaac, Sr. had a daughter in 1790. This would have
been Sarah, Isaac's sister. The will of Samuel Mayo, written
in December, 1801, states that Isaac, Jr. is the oldest son of
Isaac Mayo, Sr. The will of Isaac, Sr., written on Jan. 8, 1797,
states that he has four children: Isaac, Joseph, Sarah, and
George. Thus three children were born between 1790 and Jan.,
1797, and if Isaac was the oldest, he could not have been born
in Sept., 1795. It would appear that his obituary was correct.
Isaac, Sr. owned and lived in a house on the Collersly tract,
just adjacent to the Selby's Marsh land, and it can be inferred
that Isaac Mayo, Jr. was born in that house.

As previously indicated, Isaac Mayo's father died in
1797. His mother, originally Sarah Anne Thornton, was remarried on Feb. 17, 1798, to Jonathan Waters, who lived in
the same area according to the 1800 census.[7] Jonathan Waters adopted the Mayo children on June 16, 1798. Isaac grew
up with two step-brothers born in 1799 and 1801. In Isaac's
journal of 1826-1830 he mentions another step brother named
James Lawrence Waters and a step-sister named Julianna. The
Orphan Court records indicate that Isaac was receiving income from his father's and his Uncle Samuel's estates, and
that most of the money was paid to Jonathan Waters for room
and board until 1809.[8] When Isaac entered the Navy as a
midshipman in 1809, Jonathan Waters was no longer his guardian, which would again tend to confirm that Isaac was 18 years
old at that time and that his birthday was in 1791.

Little is known about Isaac Mayo's personal life until
1833. He served on U.S. Navy ships during the entire time
except for about a year in 1823-1824, 2-1/2 years in 1827-
1830 and for nearly 6 years starting in 1831. Mayo kept a
journal from June 1826 to 1830, most of which describes his

tour of Europe in 1826 and 1827. In the journal Mayo has included a small section about his family and mentions that he fought two duels with a "well-educated Austrian gentleman" who wanted to marry his half-sister, Julianna. The duels were related to Mayo's opposition to the marriage. Apparently, no one was injured and the marriage occurred. His journal for that time period also states that in the spring and summer of 1827 he was occupied in building and improving his Gresham estate. Mayo visited the springs in Maryland and Virginia in the summer of 1828 and springs in Pennsylvania in the summer of 1829. He "encountered such scenes as are usually met with in watering places, so gave no account of occurrences."[9]

Isaac Mayo mortgaged Selby's Marsh and Gresham for $8500 in March, 1820, which probably was the source of funds for his European trip. The payment schedule permitted either James Williamson, his sister's husband, or himself to make payments.[10] James Williamson was quite wealthy and a prominent citizen in Annapolis. He owned the Williamson Hotel in Annapolis in partnership with Thomas Swann. These two also owned the mail route from Baltimore and Washington to Annapolis, and James Williamson was a delegate to the State Legislature from Annapolis. It is quite probable that Isaac's sister introduced him to his future wife and promoted his marriage. James Williamson died Oct. 25, 1832, and Isaac Mayo was his executor.[11]

At this point Isaac's life took a turn for the better. First he paid off the mortgage on his Selby's Marsh land and Gresham, in Feb., 1833.[12] Next he married Sarah Battaile Fitzhugh Bland, daughter of Theodoric Bland and Sarah Davies, on Sept. 23, 1833. She was born in 1808, and was seventeen years younger than Isaac. Theodoric Bland was Chancellor of Maryland and had been Consul to Brazil. He owned property in Howard County as well as in Annapolis. Isaac was able to purchase another 256 acres of fertile farm land, called "Cotter's Desire," adjoining and just south of his Selby's Marsh land on Jan. 15, 1835, for $2927.50.[13] The money possibly came from his father-in-law. Isaac now had the start of his estate to which he added throughout his life.

Isaac Mayo's first child, Sarah Henrietta, was born on June 24, 1836, and Isaac was home for the birth. She was named after his older sister. Sarah lived only until Sept. 2, 1842, and died at about the same time that Mayo's wife's aunt, Sophia Bland died. Sophia Bland lived with the Isaac Mayo family. Her small estate consisted of some bank stock which thereafter produced income for Isaac's wife.[14] His second child, Sophia Bland Mayo, was born on Sept. 19, 1839, while Isaac was in Florida in command of the *Poinsett*. She lived until Dec. 28, 1915, and is the ancestor of all the Isaac Mayo descendants. The oldest son, Theodoric, was born in 1841 and died on Sept 26, 1843. Isaac was home for the birth but was aboard the *Macedonian* in Africa at the time of Theodoric's death. The youngest son, William Johns Mayo, was born August 18, 1846, while Isaac was home, but died on Oct. 1, 1875, after the death of his father.[15] Thus, Isaac Mayo's family life had much sadness in it.

Isaac was appointed executor of two large estates during his lifetime. The first estate was that of his sister's husband, James Williamson. Mayo requested in his letter to the Secretary of the Navy in Oct., 1837, that he be relieved of his command of *USS Fairfield* on the Brazil Station in April, 1838, so that he could settle the estate which "amounted to $30,000."[16] The second estate, that of his father-in-law, Theodoric Bland, also required that he ask for relief of his duties aboard ship to attend to personal business. In this instance Mayo was detached from his command during the Mexican War, *USS Mississippi*, on July 19, 1847.

Theodoric Bland had died on Nov. 16, 1846, and his will named Captain Isaac Mayo as his executor.[17] There was a considerable amount of property and money involved, including real estate in Virginia and Maryland. Theodoric's widow, his son, William Glenn Bland, and his daughter, Sarah B.F. Mayo, survived him. The will made provision for the widow and son, then left the remainder to Isaac's wife and children. All of William's property was also to go to Isaac's wife and children after William's death. William had been thrown from a horse when he was at Cambridge College, near Boston. The fall injured his head to the extent that he was not capable. Isaac was later appointed his trustee. Apparently, Isaac Mayo benefited greatly from these inheritances, as he had from those of his father and his uncle earlier in his life. Surely, these shortened tours had some effect on Mayo's military career, but it is difficult to assess.

Various letters, articles and portions of books written during Mayo's lifetime help describe his personality and character. His obituary states, "In private life he was kind, courteous and affable, a thoughtful neighbor, a considerate and attentive master, a devoted husband and father."[18] A description of Mayo aboard ship characterizes Mayo: "Our Commander, Isaac Mayo of Annapolis, Maryland, was a brave and skillful officer. Courteous to all under his command, he never allowed any officer to use opprobrious language to the most humble individual in the ship. The men were never denied access to him, and they were sure to have their wrongs redressed by making them known to Capt. Mayo. He commanded the *Fairfield* during the eighteen months succeeding her departure from the United States. He was then relieved and returned home; and so great was the regret of the ship's company on his leaving, that from the oldest seaman to the smallest boy in the ship, there was a general gloom of countenance. Some of the old salts' that had braved every clime from the Arctic to the Antarctic, 'piped their eye' and said 'we have lost our father.' This may seem romance, yet it is true. It is with much pleasure I record this trifling tribute to his worth."[19]

A local newspaper reported his return from Mexico as follows: "We were delighted to witness on Tuesday evening last, the safe arrival here, of our gallant friend, Capt. Isaac Mayo, of the U. S. Navy. He looks weather-beaten, a little thin, but as young and hearty as ever. Wherever he moved, he was met by the warmest greetings."[20]

A letter from James Fenimore Cooper in February, 1850, while Mayo was visiting New York City, contains a compliment: "My dear Mayo, I called at the American soon after your arrival, left a card for Aulick, and inquired for you. You were not there, I heard you were at Brooklyn. And one Sunday I got to the door of your house, there to make a clean sweep of Read, Kearney and yourself, when they told me you were all at dinner. Here, when Shubrick called the other night, I was all set to venture into strange places. For several days I have been on the doctor's list and quite off my feed.

"Forget old friends, forsooth ho-no. My dear fellow I do nothing of a sort and I felt proud of you when General Scott told me the other night: 'Your friend Mayo is one of the bravest men I ever knew.' This was somewhat of a compliment from such a man. By the way he left a card at this house a day or two since intended for you.

"I should be sorry not to see you before you go. I shall call, but am yet so weak am to go very little out. Very Sincerely yours, J. Fenimore Cooper"[21]

One of Mayo's official letters toward the end of his tour as Commodore on the *USS Constitution* reveals that he considers himself above all, a patriot. He recounts that he had a record of 45 years in the Navy, 25 years at sea with never having a shore duty assignment. He reminds the Secretary of the Navy that he was always among the first to volunteer when there was "a speck of war on the horizon." He then states that he has no mercenary motives, in that he was rather wealthy due to his forefathers and his own management of his estates. He says that his grandfather, Joseph Mayo, sent seven sons to the Revolutionary Army and only two returned, one of whom was Isaac Mayo's father. The father's health was damaged; the other five died in the Battle of Long Island or in prisons.[22]

A private letter from Mayo at about the same time as he wrote the official letter discussed above makes it clear that he considers his Navy career to be above reproach, but concedes that he may have enemies within the Navy. He states that he was in good standing with the Navy Department. He had received the approval of the Department in all professional matters committed to his charge. He had several times received the thanks of Congress and had received a silver medal and dress sword in recognition of his service. He commented that he was well-known as having an iron constitution. Mayo then reviews possible enemies within the Navy that he may have made and says, "If I did enter my protest at the Department against an officer having a broad pennant (a Commodore) until certain reports against him were cleared up, it was my professional pride that induced me to do so. If I have rebuked another for expressing abolition notions to me in a Slave State, I was prompted to do so in defense of our Southern institutions." He also suggests that there might be some envy among his fellow officers, saying, "If it is a crime to be possessed of ample wealth to entertain and move about like a Gentleman and to present those that I esteem with a few cases of Old Madeira on my return from a cruise, I plead guilty to the charges."

In the same personal letter he recounts an incident at the election polls that illuminates several aspects of his personal life: "I was accused of having committed a political sin for having taken my tenants and managers to the polls in my carriages. On my reaching the grounds a Democratic ticket was handed to me with a caption 'I know no North, no South, no West, no East'. I jokingly remarked, 'a very poor navigator indeed not to know the cardinal points of the compass'; much mirth followed and my impression is that Col. G.W. Hughes [from Tulip Hill, five miles south of Gresham], the leading Democrat of the district, observed. Col. Hughes said, 'None but a sailor would have found that out.' I said it was a very pretty ticket. I would take it home as I had some Loco-Focos there. [Loco-Foco matches were used to light candles and Mayo could have meant he would burn the ballot]. A Whig ticket was handed to me, and said I, that is the ticket I shall vote, turning to those who had gone with me. I said you will vote as you please, and they did vote as they pleased. All, except one, voted the Democratic ticket, and he said that a sword (Seward) was a bitter pill to swallow. [Seward was a U. S. Senator from New York and a prominent anti-slavery Whig.] The two parties becoming excited, General Pierce accused of fainting and falling from his horse in battle. I had served in the Mexican War, reference was made to it. I said that I had been introduced to General Pierce by Commodore Perry after the fall of Veracruz, we had dined together. I had found his bearing that of a Gentleman and a Soldier. I had heard nothing of the sort in Mexico and should not have heard it now had Gen. Pierce not been a candidate for the Presidency. I was told I would ruin our cause, my reply was a cause deserved to be ruined if it was to be sustained by falsehood. I think Col. Hughes heard a part of all of the above." [The election was for the presidency in 1852 in which General Pierce was the Democratic nominee and General Scott the Whig nominee. Both were Army officers prominent during the Mexican War, and Mayo had a personal relationship with General Scott starting at the Battle of Veracruz. Pierce won the election in a landslide principally because the Southern Whigs believed Scott was under the influence of the anti-slavery wing of the Whig party and of Senator Seward of New York.] At the end of the letter he writes about his difficulties with the Abolitionists. He said, "There is another source from which I have been and shall always expect to be annoyed. The Abolitionists--they denounced me as unfit for the Navy because I recaptured seven out of some fifteen or more of my servants which had been enticed from me."[23]

A paragraph in his will indicates some of his personal possessions that he felt were most important in his life: "To son William, my gold mounted sword given to me by my native State of Maryland. Also the silver medal presented to me by the Congress of the United States, as the inscription sets forth for 'Patriotism and Valor'---which I prize most highly and hope my son will continue to do the same---Also to my son William all my arms of every description, my curios, journals, and papers. Also my Library, most of which was given to me by my son's grandfather, the late Chancellor Bland of Maryland, as a mark of his respect."[24]

These descriptions show that Isaac Mayo was a patriot; proud of his heritage and his accomplishments, both in accumulating his estate and in the Navy; considerate and humane in his dealings with his Navy crews and with his tenants; anxious to do his duty and willing to take professional and personal risks.

There is uncertainty about the death of Mayo that lingers today. Isaac Mayo wrote his will on Dec. 26, 1860, about five months before his death.[25] This would suggest that he was not well and was preparing for the possibility of death. His sister, Sarah, died about two weeks later, and perhaps her condition caused him to prepare his will. Early in the spring of 1861 Maryland was occupied by Federal troops, and martial law was established in some localities. On May 1st, 1861, Isaac Mayo tendered his resignation from the U.S. Navy. The following is his entire letter:[26]

> Gresham
> South River, A.A. Co., Md.
> May 1st, 1861

To His Excellency Abraham Lincoln,
        President of the United States
Sir:
        I hereby most respectfully tender to you my resignation of the office of Captain in the United States Navy.

        For more than *half a century* it has been the pride of my life to hold office under the Government of the United States. For *twenty-five years* I have been engaged in active service and have *never* seen my flag dishonored or the American arms disgraced by defeat. It was the hope of my old age that I might die, as I had lived, an officer in the Navy of a free Government. This hope has been taken from me.

        In adopting the policy of *coercion*, you have denied to millions of freemen the rights of the Constitution. In its stead you have placed the *will* of a *sectional party*, and now demand submission in the name of an armed force. As one of the oldest soldiers of America, I protest--in the name of humanity--against this "war against brethren." I cannot fight *against* the Constitution while pretending to fight *for it*.

        You will, therefore, oblige me by accepting my resignation.

Most Respectfully,
Isaac Mayo
Captain U. S. Navy
Late Commander in Chief of U.S.
Naval Forces, Coast of Africa,
Constitution, flagship

The reverse notation on the Mayo letter is "Dismiss by order the President," then, "Done May 18, 1861." Abraham Lincoln's dismissal of Isaac Mayo was to be effective on May 18, 1861; however he may have been dead before the notice of dismissal could have been delivered. His monument in the Naval Academy Cemetery, erected by his wife, says he died on May 10th, 1861, while the church records say he died May 18th, 1861.

Because the date of dismissal and the date of death may have been on the same day, there has been speculation that he committed suicide after receiving the news of the dismissal There is a statement in a memorandum written September 7, 1977, to the Assistant Secretary of the Navy from his Special Assistant for Military Law regarding the naval record of Commodore Mayo in which he stated that Isaac Mayo died from a self-inflicted gunshot. A later Navy memorandum identifies Ms. Jacobsen, Maryland State Archives, as the source, and that she was merely stating folklore. No death records exist in Maryland for that period except as contained in the church records. Church records and newspaper accounts of Mayo's death contain no hint of suicide.

It is doubtful that dismissal would have been the cause of suicide. Mayo could not have been too surprised at the result of his resignation. Four other active Navy Captains had been dismissed between April 19 and April 22 after tendering their resignations. One of those was Franklin Buchanan, whom Mayo had served with and who was a friend. In that same time frame there had been three other active duty Captains who had resigned, and their resignations had been accepted, so perhaps he was hoping for a better result.27

In considering whether or not there was a suicide, there are the following factors: (1) He had made out his will just five months before as if he were anticipating death, (2) In his letter of resignation, he mentions old age and death as if it is on his mind. (3) Other active Navy Captains had been dismissed just prior to his resignation. (4) The burial location in St. Anne's Cemetery in Annapolis is unmarked, consistent with church policy at that time for a suicide. (5) An article in the Baltimore Sun on May 24th about his death indicates that "the unhappy condition of the country deeply affected him, and probably hastened his death." These factors indicate a possibility of suicide, but, of course, we will never know.

Isaac Mayo's great-great grandson wrote to the Board for Correction of Naval Records (BCNR) in April, 1976, seeking a change in the service record of Isaac Mayo. He requested that it be changed from "dismissed" to "resignation accepted." The basis for the requested change was stated to be "his naval record, advanced age and the procedurally disparate treatment, resulting in an injustice." The BCNR reviewed the information submitted and on July 22, 1977, sent a letter to the Secretary of the Navy recommending that the change in record be approved. The Executive Assistant to Mr. Hidalgo was able to muddy the waters by writing to the Director, Naval Historical Center on September 8, 1977, suggesting that the action could have an adverse impact upon historical records, constitute rewriting of history and open the way for a flood of such historical corrections. Naturally, the Director of the Naval Historical Center, wrote back on September 16, 1977, agreeing completely The next record is a letter on May 12, 1980, to Mr. Hidalgo from the same Director, Naval Historical Center reiterating his objections. The technique of writing memoranda back and forth to each other, employed by the various staff officers, is a time-honored tradition in Washington, D.C., and avoids decisions on any subject. The Asst. Secretary of the Navy returned the proceedings to the BCNR on July 23, 1980, and asked them to reconsider. On October 3, 1980, the BCNR recommended that Isaac Mayo's naval record be corrected to show that he was not dismissed from the Naval Service, but died while on the rolls of the Navy. This recommendation was based on the conclusion that he did not receive notice, either actual or constructive, of the action of the President. before he died. They referred to Winthrop's Military Law, 1866 as authority and concluded that he was dead before the official notification that he had been dismissed could arrive. He lived in a rural area and May 18th was a Saturday, so that it would have been unlikely that he would have received an official notification of dismissal. If he were dead before the official notification was received, he would have died while on active duty and could not have been dismissed. Regardless, the Asst Secretary of the Navy, John Herrington, disapproved the BCNR recommendation on February 18, 1983, stating that there was no substantial evidence that he did not receive notification.28

As part of a review of many closed cases, the case was reopened on April 3, 1990, with a request that the date of death be established with reliable evidence and that his family be asked about their understanding of the events leading to his death. The BCNR then did a thorough investigation and reported their findings to the Asst. Secretary of the Navy on March 3, 1995, in an eleven page, single-spaced memorandum. The BCNR discussed several factors that would indicate that he died on May 10th, (the date on the monument was provided by his wife, the likelihood that the Naval Academy would have verified the monument information, the difficulty of arranging a funeral and burial in two days between May 18th and May 20th and the possibility she was trying to hide a suicide). Considerations that his death was on May 18th included the usual reliability of church records. The BCNR concluded that Mayo could not have been informed of his dismissal by the time of his death; and that if he committed suicide, it wouldn't have been because of his dismissal at the hands of a man that he regarded as little more than a would-be dictator. On April 11, 1997, the Asst. Secretary of the Navy disapproved the BCNR recommendation because there was insufficient evidence to show that there was a failure to provide proper notice.

It almost seems appropriate that there is uncertainty about where Isaac Mayo is buried, with so many other uncertainties about his life. His obituary says that he was buried with the services of the Episcopal Church, and his remains were placed in the family vault in Annapolis. The old Vestry Book of All Hallows Church contains the notation that he died on May 18, 1861, and was buried in the family vault in Annapolis on May 20th. The family vault is in St. Anne's Cemetery on Northwest Street in Annapolis and has no inscription for Mayo or his wife. A tall memorial monument was erected later at a high point in the Naval Academy cemetery by his widow within direct view of the Mayo vault in St Anne's Cemetery. The records of the Naval Academy cemetery do not indicate that his remains were moved there; it states that there is a monument only. There is one account in a book written about Annapolis in 1937 that would indicate he is buried in the Naval Academy Cemetery: "Visitors to the Naval Academy cemetery will see a tall granite obelisk bearing the name 'Mayo,' which marks his resting place. At his burial service the local clergyman took advantage of the occasion to expatiate on the Commodore's resignation, pointing out that he had done it in time to 'save his honor' before he died. Whereupon an extraordinary scene took place. A young officer named Flusser, born in Annapolis, but hailing from Kentucky, sprang before the assembly and over the open grave delivered himself of an impassioned speech in behalf of the Union, and intimated that the dead officer had shown a poor regard for his oath to defend his country.......The body of Flusser lies now within a few feet of the monument to Mayo, on the very spot where he stood forth to defend the Union cause over the old Commodore's grave."29

There is a nagging question. What was Flusser doing at the funeral of Isaac Mayo? The personal journals of Isaac Mayo provide the answer. This Flusser was the son of the man with whom Mayo had fought two duels before the older Flusser married Mayo's half-sister. The account of Flusser's criticism of Mayo could not be completely true. Flusser was killed in 1864 during the Civil War and the Naval Academy Cemetery was not established until 1869. Mayo's monument was not erected until after 1869. It is possible that the episode occurred in St Anne's Cemetery at the time of his first burial in the family vault.

Mrs. Mayo died on Nov. 23, 1885, in Annapolis. Church records indicate that she too was buried in St. Anne's Cemetery. Church officials indicate that at the time of Isaac Mayo's death, a person committing suicide could be buried within the confines of a church cemetery, but no inscription could appear. The most likely burial place for both Mayo and his wife, supported by actual records, would be in St. Anne's Cemetery There have been rumors that remains were moved in the early 1970s, but no confirmation has been found.

Isaac Mayo had accomplished much in his lifetime. He had started on a small farm in rural Maryland and was raised as a stepchild. At the end he had a large estate and a fine monument in one of the most honored places in his country, yet he is little recognized by history.

.

16

"Not a drum was heard, nor a funeral note,
As his corpse to the rampart we hurried,
Not a soldier discharged his farewell shot,
O'er the grave, where our hero we buried."
Death of Sir John Moore, 1808, author unknown
Isaac Mayo's Journal

Courtesy Mr. and Mrs. Leon Johnson

GRESHAM-1995

Photograph by William J. Pierson

MAYO VAULT-ST. ANNE'S CEMETERY

Photograph by William J. Pierson

MAYO MONUMENT IN NAVAL ACADEMY CEMETERY

2
War of 1812

"Where is that Barque whose stately form,
So often has dared the ruthless storm,
Of wind and war...aye Fight,
None answers none, alas: can tell,
What that gallant ship's befell,
Or bring her fate to light."
"The Hornet." Author unknown.
Isaac Mayo's Journal.

From the point of view of his naval career, Isaac Mayo was in the right place at the right time during the War of 1812. He gained valuable battle experience and built a reputation as a fierce and brave combatant during that period. In addition, he received training from and observed in action two of that war's heroes, James Lawrence and James Biddle. Mayo was warranted a Midshipman on November 15, 1809, and appointed a Midshipman on February 12, 1810. The appointment as a Midshipman was a warrant signed by the President of the United States stating that Mayo was to follow orders of his superiors and that others under his command were to be obedient to his orders. He was not a commissioned officer until he was appointed a Lieutenant. Isaac Mayo was commissioned a Lieutenant on February 14, 1815, after only five years of service, apparently a rare occurrence in those years of the Navy.[1]

Midshipman Mayo reported to the *USS Wasp* in New York City on February 12, 1810. The *Wasp* was commanded by Lieutenant James Lawrence. Generally, the ships in the U. S. Navy in New York at that time patrolled between Montauk Point, Nantucket, Buzzards Bay and Newport, watching for British impressments and taking soundings in order to improve the charts-- not a very thrilling duty. On July 3, 1810, James Lawrence, with the 10 officers and 186 men of his crew from the *Wasp*, traded ships with the brig, *Argus*. Included in the 10 officers from the *Wasp* were five Midshipmen, one of which was Isaac Mayo. The *Argus* was employed doing much the same thing as the *Wasp*, but patrolled along the coast from New York to the Chesapeake. She also served as a target for a torpedo invented by Robert Fulton in New York. She was in Annapolis in late April and May, 1811, so that Mayo probably was able to go home. Orders were issued on May 6, 1811, to proceed to New York to execute orders for the protection of the commerce of the United States. French and British cruisers off that port were interrupting its trade. The little fleet, under the command of Commodore John Rodgers, consisted of the *President* and the *Argus*.[2] It was during this trip that the *President* battled the British *Little Belt* on May 15, 1811.

Lawrence, now a Master Commandant, took command of the *Hornet* on October 25, 1811, in Norfolk, and Isaac Mayo was transferred with him. At that time *Hornet* was a single deck man-of-war brig of 460 tons and carried 18 thirty-two pounder guns. Her mean draft was about 13 feet and her crew totaled 186 men. *Hornet* was ordered to carry dispatches to France and England and to return with the replies. The dispatches were related to impressment disputes which were leading to war with the British. The *Hornet* sailed from New York on Dec 6th, 1811, and had on board messengers to the Courts of St. Cloud (France) and St. James (Britain), Mr. Biddle and Mr. Taylor.

This trip must have been an exciting one for Midshipman Mayo. All of the eyes of the country were on *Hornet*. War fever ran high, and the replies to these dispatches could determine the course of history. The ship was visiting France and Britain. It is known that one of the midshipmen on the ship (not Mayo) accompanied the U. S. envoy to Paris, so undoubtedly the young man from rural Maryland also got a taste of the European life. The *Hornet* remained in Europe making a couple of trips between Cherbourg, France, and Cowes, England, carrying diplomatic messages. Finally, on April 27th, it set sail for the United States with Mr. Taylor, Sir James Jay, and Mr. Legrand. She made the passage in twenty-two days, suffering the loss of the foretopmast and several spars in heavy weather. The messages were received in Washington on May 22nd. They were determined to be unfavorable, and there was a tremendous outcry for war with Britain.[3]

War with England was declared on June 18th, 1812. War was made inevitable by the insolent conduct of English naval officers on the American coast. They bullied, impressed, blockaded, burned and captured as suited their caprice. At the beginning of the war the United States Navy had 17 vessels totaling 15,300 tons; the English Navy consisted of 1,048 vessels with a total tonnage of 860,990 tons. The U.S. ships had heavier hulls and proved faster, but had inferior ordnance compared to the English ships. The weak link for the English was their sea commerce, which the Americans exploited almost immediately. Hundreds of privateers were sent out and captured hundreds of English ships.[4]

At the beginning of the war the *Hornet* with Midshipman Mayo aboard, and commanded by James Lawrence, was in New

York harbor with *President*, flagship of Commodore Rodgers; *United States*, Captain Decatur; *Congress*, Captain John Smith; and *Argus*, Master Commandant Arthur Sinclair. On June 21, 1812, this fleet left New York, went to the West Indies, back across the Atlantic to the English Channel, across the banks of Newfoundland and returned to Boston on August 31st. The *Hornet* captured the English brig, *Dolphin*, on July 11th, the letter of marque, *John*, two weeks later and the brig, *Argus*, on August 2nd.[5] During this rather uneventful cruise for *Hornet*, the *Constitution* had fought the *Guerriere*. James Lawrence in the *Hornet* was impatient for a big battle on the high seas with a British warship and Midshipman Mayo, who had been aboard ship for two-and-a-half years, was a valuable member of the crew.

On October 28, 1812, a squadron under Commodore Bainbridge, consisting of the *Constitution* and the *Hornet*, left Boston and reached San Salvador on December 15th. *Hornet* was sent into the harbor and found the English sloop-of-war, the *Bonne Citoyenne*, an old French prize, undergoing repairs. Lawrence did everything in his power to provoke a battle with the slightly more powerful ship. He asked the American consul to invite the ship to battle; he passed around the harbor as a challenge; finally the *Constitution* and *Hornet* blockaded the port. The *Bonne Citoyenne* declined to fight because they felt the *Constitution* would help the *Hornet*, even though the Americans pledged that they would not do so. The *Constitution* even went so far as to anchor in the harbor to demonstrate that it would not interfere. The affair excited widespread interest in both the United States and England. The *Constitution* left San Salvador on December 26th, leaving the *Hornet* to blockade alone. Three days later the *Constitution* fought and destroyed the English frigate, *Java*. The *William* had been captured by the *Java* and now accompanied the *Constitu-*

tion back to San Salvador. It had an English crew aboard and attempted to escape. The *Hornet* recaptured it The *Constitution* sailed for Boston on January 6, 1813, and again left the *Hornet* to continue the blockade. On that day the *Hornet* captured a small English schooner, *Ellen.* It was found to have a valuable cargo.[6] According to the account of Isaac Mayo, he was appointed prizemaster. He ran into San Salvador for supplies. Thirty soldiers were sent aboard to prevent smuggling. Mayo found out from an American who came aboard that they intended to seize the ship. Mayo made a rush with his few men; drove the soldiers off the ship and then got the *Ellen* underway.[7] The ship was the best prize taken during the war and was afterward sold for $32,675 in Newcastle, Delaware.[8] On January 24th the *Montagu,* a large ship of 74 guns, arrived off San Salvador. *Hornet* escaped capture by running in towards port and at night, standing out to sea again.[9]

   Hornet then ran north with the intent of returning to the United States. On February 4, 1813, they captured the English brig *Resolution* armed with ten guns, loaded with coffee and $23,000 in silver. Lawrence removed the cargo and sank the ship. Ten days later *Hornet* sighted the English man-of-war brig *Espiegle* anchored and started toward her when they saw a sail on the horizon. This proved to be the English sloop *Peacock.* The *Hornet* headed toward *Peacock,* and both prepared for action. At 5:25 PM the two vessels passed close to each other and exchanged broadsides, *Hornet* then maneuvered into a favorable position and maintained a steady fire such that in 15 minutes the *Peacock* surrendered. Attempts were made to save the *Peacock* and her crew. Most of the crew were saved, but the *Peacock* sank, carrying with her three of the *Hornet's* crew and thirteen of the *Peacock's.* During the battle, Midshipman Mayo received severe burns on his legs from an explosion of gun powder from the enemy's guns.

The *Hornet* then prepared for a second battle with the *Espiegle* that lay within eyesight of the *Peacock* encounter, but that ship did not attempt any action. Mayo, in his account, states that the *Hornet* fired guns of defiance, but the *Espiegle* ran under the guns of nearby Demerara. The *Hornet* got underway for the United States crowded with captured crews from several different ships, short of water and food. The Commanding Officer of the *Espiegle* later received a court martial for his failure to attack the *Hornet*. The *Peacock* action attracted a lot of attention in the United States as the first sloop duel of the war. *Hornet* arrived in New York on March 24, 1813, returned from a cruise of one hundred and forty-five days, during which they had captured one ship, two brigs, one schooner and one man-of-war, an unparalleled record.[10] Lawrence became a naval hero, and undoubtedly Midshipman Mayo yearned to do the same in his career.

There is some uncertainty about the sequence of events regarding Isaac Mayo's presence on both the *Ellen*, as prizemaster, and aboard *Hornet* during the battle with *Peacock*. Mayo clearly states in his summary of his naval career that he was present for both events. The *Ellen* was captured on Jan. 6, 1813, was sent to San Salvador for supplies, then sailed to Newcastle, Delaware. *Hornet* escaped *Montagu* on Jan. 24th by running into port at San Salvador, then immediately going out to sea at night. The battle with the *Peacock* occurred on Feb 4th. For Mayo to have been on *Ellen* as prizemaster and be aboard *Hornet* for the *Peacock* battle, he would have had to transfer back to the *Hornet* in San Salvador before the *Ellen* left for Delaware. This appears feasible since the *Hornet* remained in the area at least until Jan. 24th. This sequence of events is somewhat supported by the letter that James Lawrence wrote reporting the *Hornet-Peacock* battle results. In the letter he said his sailing master and seven crew were not aboard during the conflict; they were delivering a prize to the United States. The roster of the *Hornet* crew at that time lists the sailing master as Midshipman William L. Cox; Midshipman Mayo is listed as Masters Mate.[11]

Congress authorized $25,000 to be distributed as prize money "to Captain James Lawrence, late of the sloop-of-war *Hornet*, his officers and crew or their widows and children" on July 13, 1813. On April 6th of the same year the New York City Common Council gave a dinner for the officers and crew of the *Hornet* which was preceded by a parade of the crew and an "elegant" band. The parade started at Whitehall and proceeded up to Broadway to Washington Hall where the dinner was given. The petty officers, seamen and marines were served in the Ball Room, "the most splendid room on the continent," and the officers along with various dignitaries were served in a dining room on the first floor. The rooms were decorated with paintings of the naval victories and achievements of "our gallant commanders."[12] It was thus an exciting time for Midshipman Mayo.

Captain Lawrence was too senior to remain in command of the small *Hornet*. He was relieved by Master Commandant James Biddle and transferred to command of the *Chesapeake* on about May 1, 1813. Fortunately, Midshipman Isaac Mayo remained on the *Hornet*, as did most of the other officers and crew. On June 1, 1813, the *Chesapeake* was defeated in a battle with the English ship *Shannon*, and Captain James Lawrence, along with several other officers and midshipmen, was killed. The *Chesapeake* crew was poorly trained, whereas the *Shannon* was among the best in the English fleet. It was in this battle that James Lawrence said, "Don't give up the ship" just before he died.[13]

The *Hornet* was now assigned to the squadron commanded by Stephen Decatur and consisting of the *United States*, *Macedonian* and *Hornet* stationed in New York City. In late May, 1813, they attempted to go to sea from New York by way of Long Island Sound. Just outside the sound they encountered British ships, consisting of two ships of the line, along with frigates. They were chased by the British ships and had to run back to New London. The British force soon increased to seven ships of the line and frigates, trapping the Americans. Mayo reported that the *Hornet* narrowly escaped capture on that trip. The three American ships sailed eight miles up the Thames where they found the protection of earthworks, as well as by a chain across the river entrance. The location was facetiously called by local residents, "Fort Decatur." In December, 1813, they tried to escape, but Decatur called it off after observing signals from along the shore alerting the British blockading force.[14]

In January, 1814, Biddle was selected to go aboard the British flagship to negotiate some individual ship combat. He became very excited about the prospect of the *Hornet* meeting his old ship, *Wasp*, now named *HMS Loup Cervier* ("Lynx"). Biddle and her captain exchanged letters on terms for the battle, but Decatur was reluctant unless the *Hornet* crew was augmented by picked officers and men from his squadron. Biddle then offered to remove his two-gun advantage and proposed that both ships fight with their normal complements. This proposal seemed satisfactory to all concerned, but before the fighting could start the *Loup Cervier* was ordered to another assignment. Isaac Mayo's report of service for that period states that he volunteered for the *Argus* (not the *Hornet*) to give battle to the *Loup Cervier* in Long Island Sound.[15] His naming of the

Argus is probably a mistake, since his account of service was written 40 years later. He also states in his report of service that he volunteered under Decatur for the defense of Washington and under Biddle for battle on the Connecticut River[16] Apparently, no action occurred as a result of these organizing efforts.

Late in December, 1814, the *Hornet*, with Isaac Mayo aboard, left New London, running in heavy weather through the blockading squadron, and went into New York. There the *President*, Commodore Decatur, the *Peacock*, Capt. Warrington, with the brig *Tom Bowline*, were assembled for a cruise to the East Indies. On January 15, 1815, the *President* left port in a snow storm to attempt to evade the blockade, but ran aground taking some damage and was eventually captured by the English blockading squadron. The remainder of the squadron was unaware of the *President*'s fate and on January 22nd ran by the blockaders in a strong northwesterly gale. The ships proceeded toward Tristan d'Acunha, which was the appointed rendezvous with *President*. In a few days the *Hornet* parted company with the other two. A few days out of Tristan, *Hornet* met a merchant ship that told him the war was over; however, Biddle did not believe him or chose not to believe him. During this trip on February 15, 1815, Isaac Mayo was promoted to Lieutenant, USN. The *Peacock* and the *Tom Bowline* arrived at Tristan d'Acunha on March 18th, and the *Hornet* arrived March 23rd. Just as the *Hornet* was about to anchor she saw a strange sail. *Hornet* pursued and caught the English ship, *Penguin*. The ships ran on the same tack, closing and firing broadsides for about 15 minutes. The *Penguin* then attempted to run into the *Hornet* and its bowsprit came in between Hornet's main and mizzen rigging. Neither ship attempted to board the other. The Captain of the English ship was killed, and Capt Biddle of the *Hornet* was wounded in the neck. The *Hornet* forged ahead tearing off the *Penguin's* foremast and bowsprit. The *Hornet* then fired another broadside, and the *Penguin* struck her colors, twenty-two minutes after the battle had begun.[17] In his history of the War of 1812 Theodore Roosevelt wrote of the battle, "Hardly any action of the war reflected greater credit on the United States marine than this; for the cool, skillful seamanship and excellent gunnery that enabled the Americans to destroy an antagonist of equal force in such an exceedingly short time."[18] The *Penguin* was so badly damaged that she had to be sunk. The prisoners were put aboard the *Tom Bowline* and sent to Rio de Janeiro.

The treaty of peace between the United States and Great Britain was signed in Ghent, Dec. 24, 1814, and ratified in Washington, Feb. 18, 1815; however, neither the English or American ships at sea were aware of it. Finally, on April 13th the *Peacock* and *Hornet*, giving up on the *President*, set sail for the East Indies. On April, 27, 1815, the two ships met the English line-of-battle warship, *Cornwallis*, at sea. The English ship was very fast and very powerful, with 74 guns. The *Peacock* was faster than the *Hornet*, so the *Cornwallis* pursued the *Hornet*. The *Hornet* first threw overboard the stores taken from the *Penguin*, and after being fired upon, she jettisoned the anchor, shot, ballast, six guns, cables and the launch. Still the *Cornwallis* closed and hit the *Hornet* hull with three shots. At that point the *Hornet* threw everything overboard that could be moved, including all guns, except one, shot and boats. At that point the wind shifted, and the *Hornet* was able to gain ground. Finally, after 48 hours of chase, the English ship turned back. The *Hornet* sailed for New York and reached there on June 9, 1815.[19]

Captain Biddle's report of the battle with *Penguin*, forwarded to the Secretary of the Navy on March 25, 1815, highly commended Isaac Mayo and stated that he had been put in charge of the *Penguin* following her surrender. His commendation included three other officers in addition to Mayo and specifically stated, "It is a most pleasing part of my duty to acquaint you, that the conduct (of the officers), I have the honor to command, was in the highest degree creditable to them, and calls for my warmest recommendation."[20] In recognition of this service Mayo received a silver medal commissioned by the Congress of the United States on February 10, 1821. Congress also appropriated $25,000 for the destruction of the *Penguin* in lieu of prize money; Mayo's share as a Lieutenant would have been significant.

In the Archives of Maryland, Resolution 61, Acts of 1827, the Legislature of the State authorized the Governor of Maryland to procure and present to Lieutenant Isaac Mayo a dress sword, suitably inscribed in recognition of his service in the War of 1812 as a testimony of the appreciation of his native state. The resolution reads in part as follows: "Resolved, unanimously, That the General Assembly of Maryland, entertain a high sense of the gallantry of Isaac Mayo, a native of this state, a lieutenant in the navy of the United States, and who participated in two brilliant and well fought actions during the late war, both of which terminated in glorious victory, viz.: the action between the United States sloop of war *Hornet*, commanded by Captain Lawrence, and the British sloop of war *Peacock*, Captain Peake, and between the *Hornet*, Captain Biddle, and the *Penguin*, Captain Dickinson, and was among those officers who received medals from the United States, as a testimony of their country's approbation." A letter from Thomas Fletcher, craftsman of Philadelphia, November 19, 1828, places the cost of the sword at $400.[21]

A description of Isaac Mayo's silver medal and sword are contained in a booklet advertising an auction on November 20, 1989. The medal is described as 2-1/2" in diameter, hand engraved on the outer rim, "The Congress U.S. to Lieut. Isaac Mayo for his Gallantry, Good Conduct and Services." The front had a bust of James Biddle, Commanding Officer of *Hornet*; the reverse side had a relief design of the naval engagement between the two vessels with the words "Capture of the British ship Penguin by U.S. ship, Hornet." All officers on the Hornet at that time received the medal; Biddle's was gold, and the others received silver. The sword is described as having a delicate hilt of solid gold with finials of full eagle heads. The straight 27" blade is etched in detailed segments depicting naval engagements of the USS Hornet, including "Peacock and Hornet 1814," "Escape of the Hornet from the Cornwallis 1815" with etchings of both ships, and details of the ships *Hornet* and *Penguin*.[22] A more complete description of both the sword and silver medal are included in Appendix D. The sword and medal were purchased and are in private hands.

Lt. Isaac Mayo remained in *Hornet* for several more years, until June 9, 1820, in peace-time service. The ship was under the command of Capt. Read during that time. They visited the West Indies and northern Europe. After Mayo became 1st Lieutenant of Hornet, they were engaged in running between the United States and Cadiz negotiating the Florida Treaty.[23]

There is a report about Isaac Mayo in the Maryland Republican for December 21, 1819, while he was serving in the *Hornet* as 1st Lieutenant, "A seaman of the United States Ship of War, *Hornet*, while ascending the main rigging to assist in sending down the topsail yard, fell from the shrouds, struck his head upon the chain stowage of the ship and fell overboard.

Lieutenant Mayo, first Lieutenant of the ship, saw his perilous situation from the quarterdeck and notwithstanding the severity of the weather, plunged in to save him, succeeded in getting him aboard; but the poor sailor was so decidedly injured that he survived but a few moments. Here indeed is a noble human spirit, one of the highest officers of a national ship beholding the situation of a dying seaman struggling with the waves. Forgetting all the distinctions of rank and authority, remembering only the duties of the man and obeying the generous impulse of his own heart, leaps into the icy cold element to his rescue. Such an act deserves a national monument--it should be perpetuated. At least we hope it will not escape the attention of the Government. And that the Navy Department will notice Lieutenant Mayo in such ways as to encourage sentiments similar to his among all our officers. With such a spirit universally in the American Navy, it must be invincible." A handwritten note indicates that this article was based on a similar article in the New York papers.[24]

We know what Mayo thought of his service in the War of 1812 from a letter written in December, 1836, to the Secretary of the Navy requesting a command. He wrote, "by reference to documents found in the Department it will be found that my service in the late War with Great Britain was, I think, equal to almost any officer of my grade of the day."[25]

Navy Museum

HORNET CLASS SLOOP

Courtesy of Beverley R. Robinson Collection, U.S. Naval Academy

THE HORNET SINKING THE PEACOCK

A. Bowen

Courtesy of Beverley R. Robinson Collection, U. S. Naval Academy

THE HORNET AND PENGUIN

A. Bowen

Naval Monument

THE HORNET'S ESCAPE FROM THE CORNWALLIS

3

USS North Carolina in the Mediterranean 1825-1827

"As pensive this night on my sea chest I lay,
Which serves me for bed, chair and table,
I mourn'd the sad hour I was placed on half pay
Without towline, or anchor or cable."
"The Lieutenant's Complaint"
Isaac Mayo's Journal

Lieutenant Isaac Mayo reported aboard the *USS North Carolina* in November, 1825. Mayo had traveled to the Mediterranean as the Maryland representative aboard the *USS Brandywine* that was returning Lafayette to France after his triumphant tour to the United States. The *Brandywine* had been named, launched, and equipped for this service and the officers selected so there would be at least one from each state. The *Brandywine* landed Lafayette, Commodore Charles Morris, and Captain G.C. Read at Le Havre before proceeding south to join the Mediterranean Fleet in Port Mahon, Island of Minorca.[1] The *North Carolina* had arrived in Gibraltar in April, 1825. Between April and November the ship had visited Malaga, Tangier, Tunis, the Aegean Sea ports of Poros and Smyrna and the Greek port of Nauplia.[2]

The *North Carolina* was a new ship and the pride of the Navy. It was 196 feet long overall with a 33-foot beam, carried 102 guns, and had a complement of 832 men. Her main yard was 124 feet long, and her main truck reached 225 feet above the waterline. The *North Carolina* was square-rigged, with each of her three masts carrying a lower course, topsail, topgallant, and royal. There were fore-and-aft spencer and spankers on the main and mizzen, many trysails, jibs, staysails and studdingsails.[3] Under full sail, the *North Carolina* was a beautiful ship. She served as the flagship for Commodore John Rodgers, the senior naval officer on active duty, whose home was in Havre de Grace, Maryland. Rodgers, a fifty-three years old career officer, had a reputation for rigid discipline. Discipline was needed, apparently, since junior officers on Mediterranean duty had "lately disgraced the country by dissipation, brawls with foreigners ashore and lethal duels among themselves." Lieutenant Matthew Calbraith Perry, who was to play such an important role in Isaac Mayo's naval career, was the First Lieutenant (second in command) of the *North Carolina*. Just before Mayo reported aboard, Captain Patterson, the Commanding Officer, was detached to take command of the *Constitution*, and Matthew Perry became the Acting Commander.[4]

The subsequent Mediterranean cruise under Commodore Rodgers was undertaken for several reasons: peace had been disturbed by a war between Algiers and Great Britain and by the Greek Revolution, and the area of the sea around Greece was infested with pirates who threatened the American trade. Most important, however, was the desire to make a treaty with Turkey; it was thought that Commodore Rodgers and a large fleet would greatly facilitate that treaty.[5]

While on this cruise Isaac Mayo observed and participated in the running of a "taut ship" through application of the
"Rodgers method" of discipline. Flogging with a cat-o'nine-
tails was an essential part of the method. This type of punish-
ment, derived from the British Royal Navy, was common to
all navies and merchant marines to the middle of the nineteenth century. Most naval officers considered flogging necessary because of the type of seamen they received aboard
their ships, which in turn stemmed from available men and
means of "hiring" them.

The recruitment methods were similar to the British
and earlier U.S. Navy practice. A new crew was enlisted for
each vessel before a deployment. The term of enlistment was
two years for boys and three for men. After return from an
extended cruise, it was customary to pay off the crew, regardless of the time of enlistment. When volunteers could not be
found, ship captains resorted to paying waterfront boarding
houses to deliver drunken men to receiving ships for which
$36 per man was paid to the boarding-house keeper. This
method resulted in a large portion of the seamen being either
foreign drifters or native derelicts. Despite such dubious methods of recruiting and discipline, many fine seamen were developed and served with great honor aboard the U.S. Navy
ships.[6]

The Mediterranean Fleet spent the winter of 1825 in
Port Mahon, Minorca, a possession of Spain where the people
were very poor. Many teenage boys eager to join the U.S.
Navy to avoid draft into the Spanish Army, obtained billets as
mess attendants aboard American ships. The U.S. Navy received every facility there by arrangement with the Spanish
government. The officers were able to socialize with the local

aristocracy, but the enlisted men had a demoralizing time because it was part of the "Rodgers system" to grant them liberty very sparingly.[7]

Commodore Rodgers' orders were to protect American commerce during the war for Greek independence and to meet with His Excellency, Capudan Pasha Khosew, Lord High Admiral of the Turkish Navy, to sound him out about a treaty. The European powers had made it impossible to do business with the Turkish Sultan in Constantinople, but our emissary there had been told that a meeting between the two Naval officers might start the process. On April 10, 1826, Commodore Rodgers' squadron left Port Mahon to try to find the Turkish admiral. They called at Algiers, Tunis, Milos, Poros, and Delos and arrived at the roadstead of Vourla, twenty miles from Smyrna, on June 19th. The *North Carolina* departed Smyrna June 30th and proceeded to Tenedos. Shortly after their arrival, the Turkish fleet sailed through the Dardanelles. One of the Turkish ships, commanded by the Turkish second in command, Caputan Bey, ran aground. Commodore Rodgers sent the *Porpoise* to offer assistance. The Americans learned that Caputan Pasha was nearby, and that he would welcome a visit by Commodore Rodgers. On July 5th Capudan Pasha arrived to see his damaged ship and sent word to the American squadron that he would be glad to see Commodore Rodgers ashore the next day. The Flag Lieutenant who delivered the message indicated that the captain of the grounded vessel would probably be beheaded unless the Americans requested mercy for him.

Commodore Rodgers met with Capudan Pasha the next day and remarked that the Pasha was brawny with a grotesque figure, with a huge gray beard; and that he was dressed richly; however, he had polished manners, was polite and genteel. The Pasha mentioned that the British agents and navy officers had misrepresented America and, now that he had met Americans, he would know what to tell his sovereign, the Sultan. Commodore Rodgers did have the opportunity to tell the Pasha that he hoped Capudan Bey would not be punished with death. The Pasha replied that since Rodgers had requested it, the Capudan's life would be spared.[8]

The *North Carolina* thereafter cruised into the Dardanelles' entrance, the River Scamander, by the islands of Tenedos, Imbros, Samothrace, and Lemnos, observed Mount Ida, Mount Athos, Mount Olympus, as well as the tombs of Ajax and Achilles and Cape Baba. They anchored at the town of Mytilene. Through their stay, various salutes and formal visits were exchanged before the American fleet later left in a splash of glory. Commodore Rodgers' letter to the Secretary of the Navy described the departure: "This afternoon the squadron got underway, and after making a tack to windward, each ship bore up in succession and ran down through the Turkish Fleet, and on coming abreast of the Flag of Capudan Pasha, manned her rigging, the crew dressed in white, and gave him three cheers, the band at the same time playing 'Hail Columbia'. The exhibition of the squadron on this occasion must have been very imposing, inasmuch as the several evolutions of getting underway, of making sail, of tacking, of bearing up, of manning the rigging, and of putting the ship under a crowd of sail in a moment, as it were, after cheering, were performed each with a celerity and precision such as I have never before witnessed."[9] The diplomatic process begun at this time was culminated in 1830 when a treaty was negotiated with Turkey by Commodore James Biddle, a successor to Commodore Rodgers. Isaac Mayo had an interesting perspective on the three cheers. He said in his journal for the period that the

Turks seemed not to comprehend the three cheers. He believed that they looked upon it as something connected with the Americans mode of worship because they did not return it and the Turks give three shouts at their prayers.

The officers of the Mediterranean Squadron were greatly interested in the ancient Greek culture and sites. They were encouraged to visit the classic sites when the opportunity presented itself. Of particular interest in the life of Isaac Mayo is the island of Delos. Legend identifies Delos as the birthplace of Apollo and his twin sister Artemis. In the heart of the Aegean, tiny uninhabited Delos is still one of the most important archaeological sites in Greece. Isaac Mayo was able to bring back to his home, Gresham, remains of these ancient ruins. The bases of two marble columns still reside at Gresham in Mayo, Md. One is inscribed with the words, "From the Temple of Apollo, the Grecian Island of Delos," the other is inscribed, "From Temple of Diana." Also at Gresham one may find an old iron urn placed on a square of marble and marked "From the Island of Delos."[10] It is reported that about 1930 a descendant of Commodore M. C. Perry, the Acting Captain of the *North Carolina*, had found carved on the base of a statue of Apollo on Delos, "M.C. Perry, Captain, U.S.N., 1826."[11]

After departing the Turkish port, the *North Carolina* with their fleet went to Vourla near Smyrna, then to Port Mahon. They arrived in Port Mahon on September 10, 1826. It was here that Isaac Mayo left the ship for his tour of Europe after getting permission from Commodore Rodgers. Early in December the *North Carolina* went to Toulon and inspected the dockyards. They followed with a visit to Marseilles, where they were cordially entertained by the British

Admiral, Sir Alexander Cochrane. The ship returned to Toulon, proceeded to Tunis, then sailed toward Port Mahon. It was on this trip that misfortune fell on *North Carolina*. She encountered a violent norther with which she fought most of the month of January, 1827. For several days during the storm the ship was able only to carry close-reefed maintopsails and storm staysails; and to keep these in repair, from fifteen to eighteen sailmakers were busy night and day. Many of the officers and seamen fell ill with pulmonary diseases due to exposure and privations, and smallpox made its appearance. Finally, on exhausting their provisions, and with more than 130 officers and men on the sick list, they ran into Malta, arriving on January 20th. The British admiral received 117 of the sick at their hospital. The ship was quarantined, fumigated, scrubbed, cleaned and painted. When the ship left Malta on February 17th, nearly all patients were well and on March 3rd Commodore Rodgers reported from Port Mahon that the smallpox had disappeared and the health of the vessel was good.[12] Isaac Mayo reported aboard the *North Carolina* on March 27th after his European travel, and simply reported in his journal that smallpox "had made considerable havoc onboard, but the sick were all recovering."

The *North Carolina* received good news in Port Mahon. She was ordered home. They sailed in mid-May, stopping at Gibraltar, Cape Haitian, Port au Prince, Havana, and Key West. On July 28, 1827, she anchored in Hampton Roads.[13] Shortly after the arrival of *North Carolina* in Norfolk, Isaac Mayo was detached on August 15, 1827, and began a two-and a half-year period on leave awaiting orders.[14] On February 4, 1827, the Legislature of the State of Maryland authorized the Governor of Maryland to procure and present to Lieutenant Isaac Mayo a dress sword, suitably inscribed in recognition of his service in the War of 1812. It had only taken about 13 years![15]

Lagman

Navy Museum

USS NORTH CAROLINA IN A GALE, DECEMBER 28, 1826.

4
Travel in Europe
1826-1827

"Now I think on the time when all snugly aboard,
In the wardroom assembled together,
With plenty of wine, and a table well stored,
We laugh'd at dull care and foul weather."
"The Lieutenant's Complaint." Author unknown.
Isaac Mayo's Journal

Isaac Mayo had the opportunity to travel in Greece, Turkey, Spain, France, Switzerland, Monaco and Italy while he was assigned to the *USS North Carolina* as the Flag Lieutenant to Commodore Rodgers. His observations and adventures during his visits to those countries can be found in his private journal for that time period.[1] He visited Greece and Turkey on short tours while living aboard ship; he toured the other countries during a five-month leave of absence granted to him by the Commodore.

A Grotto on a Greek Island. "We met several hundred people who made their escape when over run by the Turks. They live sometimes upon the sea, sometimes upon the Islands. Their fate is a hard one indeed; they are driven from their homes and they say they cannot starve. They were very polite to us. They are a fine race of men; each is armed with a very long gun, a brace of pistols, an ataghan [a long knife or sabre] and a dish. We set out for the Grotto. The weather was fine and we reached the entrance at noon. Our party fortified ourselves with a drink whilst the guides were employed in securing and letting down the rope ladder by which we were to descend.

"The entrance of the grotto is not unlike that of St. Michaels cove at Gibraltar. The descent is very difficult. Each had a torch, and when we had descended to the first platform, some of the party rested for a while. The rest went on, each with one or two torches. The scenery is truly grand-the stalactites hanging from the roof down and each are seen magnificently. Also, there are pillars of every order, the most fanciful freaks of nature. This cove has been described by some as the most beautiful of all. I would advise all who may ever have an opportunity to visit this grotto. I added my name (also the names of many that I hold dear at home) to the many that were there. I could but admire a line written under the name of a lady by her husband, who says, 'Even here, I think of my very dear wife who I hope is now well in Paris.'

"Our party numbered twenty-five, including boatmen and donkey drivers, each carrying a torch, for it is as dark as pitch without them. When we had descended to the bottom and drunk from the spring, our attention was attracted by the appearance of a thousand torches and many voices from one of the upper platforms. Shouting 'Constitution,' the shout explained what at first was a mystery. Our party shouted, 'North Carolina.' Someone from above called to know if we had all the ship's company below, for it appeared to them as if we had a thousand lights. The party above were from the *Constitution* frigate. The distance between the two parties appeared at most one mile. The two parties met on the second platform. Our general shout was given, 'Huzzah America,' which was echoed throughout the immense cavern. The guides give notice upon leaving the grotto that it is extremely dangerous to explore oneself.

"The same evening we took supper and lodged at the town of Paros. Here we found large and beautiful columns of marble used in the walls of very ordinary buildings. In the old church we saw the font at which the first Christians of the island were baptized. We returned to the ship, stopping at the marble quarry from which it is supposed that most of the marble is mined."

Smyrna. "This is a large and filthy city where all nations are living in apparent harmony. The city is divided into what is called the Jew and the Turk towns. A little, dirty stream was pointed out to me; which in the time of Homer is said to have been a fine river, and where he returned, though blind, to write and study. An old church was pointed out as standing on the foundations of one of the seven churches mentioned in the Testament.

"Took a Turkish bath and the bath was near the death of me, from too sudden immersion. I would recommend all strangers who are disposed to take them, to be governed by the keepers of the bath. I took my own and was sick in bed for twenty-four hours before the perspiration could be restored. All of this time the Lady of M. Offley, consular agent at whose house I was and who is a Greek, did not leave the outer door of my apartment. I cannot be sufficiently grateful for her attention. Smyrna is seldom clear of the Plague. I have seen many carried out who died of it, but this danger is like all others. It soon becomes familiar and loses all its horrors in a few days."

Plains of Troy. "Early this morning we set out with mules and guides for the Plains of Troy. Three tombs were pointed out to us as the tombs of Achilles, Ajax and Hector. The famous rivers here are but small streams at this season. I leaped over each of them without much difficulty, but this cannot always be done, for this is the dry season. We have a fine view of the mountains in the rear of the Plains. Mount Olympus is 140 miles east of us, but not in sight. Homer is the author for the existence of a Troy. The traces of a city are only visible in the broken rocks that are yet to be seen scattered over the Plains. The Plains are several leagues wide. Some parts of it are in cultivation, but much of it is grown up in woods, of small growth, except the oak which is large. The acorns are collected and said to be used for food.

"The marble from old Troy has been mostly taken away to build other cities, and probably much of it in building Alexandria Troyas. That city was built by Alexander the Great and now is in ruins. The ruins of a palace was pointed out to us and is called Prians, but it seems contemporary with the city. Took Homer's *Iliad* with me upon the Plains and the situation of the islands is accurately described as well as some points in Greece. Drank waters of Scamander and washed my face in them. Purchased an outer robe from the graceful shoulders of a Trojan dame or damsel of Grecian descent. The Turkish women seldom show their faces. Purchased a copper finger ring from an old Turk. Dined with a Mussulman who very soon became intoxicated. Everything with which a Turk is at all associated appears to be in a state of dilapidation. They never repair their houses. The sail, when worked from the land, is never repaired. The millions of grasshoppers upon the Plains are far beyond calculation or belief unless to those who have actually seen them."

Town of Mytilene. "Went ashore to witness the treatment that the Greeks receive from the Turks. They slit them with the sides of their Ataghan; the poor Greek with his hands upon his breast hangs his head in shame. Procured a complete Greek dress. The costume is graceful, and I think the most natural of any other nation. The only curiosity or antique I saw was a stone chair used by the ancient. Lord Byron resided here some time."

Milo. "Bathed in the subterranean springs of Milo. They are a few hundred yards from the shore and are entered with lighted torches. It has an exit into the harbor where the water is so warm that one cannot remain there any time in it. Took a digging party to ancient Milo. Got many specimens such as the marble and stone seats of the Senators. Both have been buried for ages, only having been observed within the last few years. Both natives and strangers make it a business to dig for curiosities at the tombs and catacombs. Some valuables and rare antiques have been discovered. I saw a finger very recently taken from a tomb; its weight in gold was equal to fifty-two dollars. It was sold by the pilot of the U. S. schooner *Porpoise* for two hundred dollars to an American gentleman in Smyrna. I saw a body with the arms and legs broken off. I suppose that all the statues of the heathen deities were demolished when the inhabitants embraced Christianity or by the fury of the Christians of the early ages.

"Visited several Greek families. Women are the same, kind, gentle, amiable and friendly being everywhere and he that is not well-treated by them must carry it deeply marked upon his brow. Grapes and dried fruit was set before us, with the light wine of the country. Some of the Greek women are truly beautiful, but they are not generally friendly, which is not surprising, for from their infancy up they are continually left in a high state of alarm, with the fear of being torn away from their family and friends by some merciless Aga or Pasha."

On October 15, 1826, Isaac Mayo received permission from Commodore Rodgers to tour the continent. He took passage on the packet and in twenty-one hours arrived at Barcelona, Spain, to start his tour.

Barcelona. "Barcelona is a walled city, now governed by several thousand French troops. It is tolerably well-built, most of the streets are very narrow, with the exception of one. The one very wide street and the sea wall form the Great Promenade. The population is estimated at 120,000. There are no very substantial buildings, except for the custom house. It has twelve churches and fifty convents. It had many more, but a number were suppressed during the time of the Constitution. The population of the city and most of Catalonia are decidedly in favor of the Constitution."

Travel to France. "To get my passport to France I had to pay five francs as a fee. When I asked why I had to pay and others did not, he said, 'Americans were rich and should be made to pay for traveling on the Continent.' Set out from Barcelona in the Diligence. The roads are only dirt, yet we are taken over them at a most rapid rate, generally by mules, and sometimes six and eight hitched to the Diligence. Crossed the rivers without a bridge. The fields are pretty well cultivated; olives, vines and wheat. The females take care of the flocks and labor in the fields in common with the men. The route in some places winds beautifully along the shore of the Mediterranean. On October 22nd, we set out from the last fort in Spain, Juan Quera, with seven small, but very spirited, horses and soon commenced ascending the Pyrenees at a full gallop, accompanied by the whooping of the conductor. Saw many Moorish castles in high places while still in Spain. At the boundary of Spain and France there is a stone on each side of the road, about ten feet high. The road over the Pyrenees is excellent. It winds up and through the mountains so as to make its ascent in no part very abrupt. At Belliguard the baggage was overhauled. The purser whose duty it was to inspect my trunk, looked first at my trunk and then at its owner. I took the hint, gave him half a franc and was saved the trouble of repacking. The Pyrenees is mostly grazed by sheep. The cork is the largest tree that I have seen growing upon the mountains. It is stripped of its bark every ninth year. Although the trunk is left naked, they are not injured."

French Countryside. "I have seen France from the Pyrenees to Paris. It does not deserve the name of La Belle France, at least I do not think so, with a few exceptions. The country is level almost to a plain, and I must complain of, and find the same fault as in Spain, which is there are no snug country houses upon the estates, which seems to me a want of civilization. The people are herded together in small, filthy towns and villages at short distances. There is not the least appearance of comfort, and their great treasure consists in the size of the heap of manure at the very threshold of the door. In the fields are seen ugly, old women attending a flock of black hogs, the girls the cattle and the boys the sheep. There are no fences so every species of stock must have a watch kept over it. The men are at the plough, which has but one handle, and it is difficult to say which way it throws the furrow. Yet, the fields are clear and well-cultivated. Heavens preserve the American farmer from such a life. Shepherds and shepherdesses lose their charms when put in practice in France and Spain, and I very much suspect in every country."

Paris. "Took four rooms in the Hotel Vivienne in Rue Vivienne, No. 14 on the seventh story, 103 steps, for which I pay seventy francs a month. The nearer a person lives to heaven in Paris, does not at all take from his respectability. Called on our minister, Mr. Brown and Lady. He appears an estimable man. Mrs. Brown is too condescending. Her manners would say, I will exert myself to make you easy in my company, for I see that you feel my superiority. This I dislike in anybody, so I make myself unusually careless. I was much pleasured to meet with my old messmate, James Fenimore Cooper, the author of the Spy. From the ministers I went home with him. The easy manner of his Lady, was much more to my American taste. Cooper and his Lady are yet very national. Subscribed to Galignani's Reading Rooms, which most Americans do. For you have American papers and can see on the register what Americans are in Paris."

Isaac Mayo visits the Exchange of Commerce, Palace of Luxembourg, Observatory, Church of St. Genevieve, Church of St. Sulpice, Palace of the Tuleries, the Louvre, Hotel Royal Des Invilides, the French and Italian Operas, Church of Notre Dame and Arch of Triumph. He devotes an entire day to each and describes in detail the measurements, arrangements, art that especially interests him, and some of the history. Much of the information seems to be from a travel guide. On November 16th, he received a note from General Lafayette as follows, " My dear Sir, I find you are in Town but do not know for how much time, and what is your destination. Yet I hope we will not be deprived of the pleasure to welcome you at La Grange, the failure of which would be a great disappointment for the whole family and particularly your sincere friend. La Fayette"

Mayo writes in his journal, "Having heard that the General was overrun by my countrymen, I had concluded to leave Paris without visiting La Grange--not withstanding my promise to his entire family a year before at Havre de Grasse."

Visit to Lafayette at La Grange. Isaac Mayo, on November 30th, traveled by carriage for a distance of about thirty miles to a place called Rosay, about one and a half miles from La Grange. He was met there by the General's carriage that then carried him to the chateau.

He wrote, " We were kindly received by the General and his numerous family, many of them I had seen and known before, having accompanied the General across the Atlantic in the *Brandywine* frigate. Several of his family met us at Le Havre. At five the family had all assembled in the drawing room and at six we descended to dinner as is customary in his house. We remained only thirty-six hours with this most charming family. [Lieutenant Goldsborough accompanied Mayo on this trip.]

"The General is never tired of doing good. As I had but recently returned from Greece, he evinced the greatest anxiety about those oppressed people and displayed the greatest interest in their welfare. The following morning the General took me over his estate and showing me the improvements he had made since his return from the United States. He took me by the hand and said, 'You see, my dear friend, how happy we are all made.' His estate consists of seven hundred acres highly improved. He pointed out a place in his barn and said, here my threshing machine is to be placed and I am only waiting for a model which Governor Sprigg of Maryland had promised to send me. I mention this incident to show how sacred he held everything connected with the United States, or its individuals.

"The internal arrangement of the General's house can but please an American. On the right wall of the first salon is suspended the American flag, which the General took with him from the *Brandywine* frigate. I had placed the flag in the possession of his granddaughter, Matilda. She reminded me of this little incident. On the right of the flag is the portrait of Washington; on the left, that of Franklin, the latter executed by one of the General's granddaughters. In the same salon is the Declaration of Independence and the Farewell Address of Washington. In the second salon are the portraits of all the Presidents of the United States. There is no parade, no ostentation in this house; as soon as entered, one feels at home. For it is immediately discovered that none is put to the least trouble, which is the greatest luxury that a visitor can enjoy.

"The second night, on retiring, we took, as we supposed, a final leave of the family, as we were to set out at daylight in the morning. But we were most agreeably disappointed, for the good old General and his son, George Washington, were already up and took breakfast with us before we set out. Mrs. George Washington La Fayette is a very intelligent lady. She is President of a Greek Female Society and has made me promise to give her all the news relative to Greece."

Return to Paris. He and Lieutenant Goldsborough returned to Paris and spent about one more week sightseeing. They went to Versailles, "decidedly the handsomest city that I have seen in France," Garden of Natural History, Gallery of Anatomy, Gallery of Botany, Menagerie of Live Animals, Library of Natural History and the Diorama. Again, he spent about one day at each location. Their final visit before Isaac Mayo's departure was to the cemetery of Pierre Le Chaise. He wrote, " I am led here more particularly to see the temporary monument to General Foy, the champion of the liberals in France and the intimate friend of our La Fayette. It is but a few months since the death of General Foy, and nine million francs already have been subscribed by the liberals of France to erect a splendid monument to his memory. The Bourbons must be trembling at this. Lieutenant Goldsborough and myself added two wreaths to the thousands already upon his grave. The French put wreaths of flowers on the tombs and graves of those they love and esteem. The effect is soothing, even to a stranger. It is one of the last tributes of respect we can pay to the deceased."

His final thoughts about Paris were, "All the world is in Paris. I will say no more about it. My curiosity is gratified. Though not particularly partial to France; yet, I love Paris. London is nothing to compare to it. Everybody is polite, cheerful, smiling in Paris, but will do nothing to help. John Bull will do much more for one and yet abuse him all the time. A Frenchman will make his thousand bows and professions, but regret that he cannot serve his dear friend upon such an occasion, but upon any other occasion will be at his service. Adieu to Paris."

Switzerland. Isaac Mayo traveled to Switzerland by carriage passing through Burgundy. He observed that all the palaces in that area were torn down during the revolution and that first rate Burgundy was "at a very low price." His final night in France was spent at Les Rouses, where the landlady would give them nothing but eggs and milk without the permission of the curate, but the snow was falling too heavily to pursue him.

Mayo traveled by sleigh to the first village in Switzerland. He wrote about the village, "The size of the village tavern reminded me of home for upon it was the words, Liberty and Country, words never met with in France or Spain. Upon the sign is a likeness of William Tell, the Swiss patriot, holding a shield in his left hand, on which are written Liberty and my Country, and in his right hand is a cross bow."

The next stage of the trip passed by Lake Geneva; he arrived at Geneva on December 9th. "I visited the house in which Jean Jacques Rousseau was born. It is now undergoing repairs and the front will be entirely new of handsome white stone. There is a small island in the Rhone which divides the stream on which is a tower serving for a clock. It stands upon the foundation of a tower erected by Julius Caesar to defend the river. There are two handsome foot bridges constructed of wire over the double ditch on the land side. The botanical garden is small. The cathedral is a handsome building; its tower affords a fine view of the lake. I visited the museum of natural history; amongst the medallions is one of Washington. Senor Abbadio, a gentleman who I knew at Panama, has just left here. Took a carriage for the chateau of Voltaire. Entered his bed chamber which is still furnished with the same articles as when he left it the last time for Paris. It is very plain and has but one window. The paintings are only tolerable; one of himself during his youth. Amongst the engravings are one of Washington and one of Franklin."

Mayo then traveled to Lausanne by steamboat. "The steamboat was built by an American by the name of Church. Landed at Lausanne and put up at the Hotel Leon D'Ore." He doesn't stay long in that city, but observes that "Should I ever be induced to live abroad, this will be the place that I should select. The schools here are said to be very superior. There are many English and other foreign youths at them."

The next stage of his journey takes him through

Switzerland towards Italy. He comments that in St. Maurice he first observed the "swelled necks." He wrote, "They are frequently idiots, called Cretins. The body becomes dwarfish, the features ugly and unintelligent." He arrived at the western edge of the Alps and wrote, "As no traveler should leave Switzerland without performing the passage of the Simplon, so I have determined to undertake it, although at a most dangerous season."

"At three in the morning set out in two-horse-tandem sleighs, for here the snow commences. The road soon became horrible; the ascent is gradual and the snow is four feet deep in the road. The weather is fine though intensely cold. At noon we reached the glacier gallery where the road is cut through a solid mountain of ice. This is near the most elevated point of the road where there is a hospital of monks of the Capuchin order. Travelers who cannot pay are entertained gratis; but such as can afford, make them presents. The monks have large dogs trained to assist travelers overtaken by snow storms and are taught to conduct them to the hospital.

"From this point of view is most awfully grand. One view looking back upon Switzerland; the other towards Italy. The glacier gallery is cut through a solid body of ice for 130 feet. The appearance in passing through is novel, but the cold too intense to remain long in it. Saw two avalanche. One of them accumulated to an immense size when plunging from a precipice and falling into the abyss. Made the very mountains tremble. After two hours of rapid descent from the summit we arrived at the village of Simplon. It is most romantically situated amongst the mountains. The inhabitants are mostly clothed in sheep skin. The scenery on the Italian side of the Alps is more bold and imposing than on the side of Switzerland. Continued down the Italian side at a rapid rate; the sleigh sometimes almost hanging over an abyss of a thousand feet. This stupendous road, which has overcome the obstructions of nature, has forty bridges thrown from one wild chasm to another and numerous subterranean passages cut through solid granite. This is Italy, and a Swiss who was in the sleigh with me put his finger upon his lips, and said, 'We are out of Switzerland. Let us talk no more of liberty and William Tell.' Soon the snow disappears; we left the sleighs and took a sidelong voiture."

Milan. Mayo traveled along Lake Como and proceeded to Milan. He visited the cathedral in Milan and was very impressed with it, writing that, "It was very far superior to any church or cathedral I have yet seen." He visited the Mint, the Amphitheater of Napoleon, witnessed a review of the Austrian troops, looked at an unfinished triumphal arch for Napoleon and went to the Escala, "said to be the largest theater in the world." He comments that he saw several operas and that "he had become delighted with the opera." Mayo deemed the paintings in the many galleries as superior and the churches magnificent. He describes Milan as rivaling Paris or London. "The streets are generally very far superior to either; being very wide-paved, sideways, and are very clean. What I have nowhere before seen, there are slabs of smooth stone or marble laid through the principal streets for the wheels of carriages to run upon. The noise of the wheels running over the pavement and jolting is obviated. One goes along as smoothly as if in a sleigh. There are one or more canals running through the city. I like the Milanese women better than the French because they are not so commercial. I could find much more to say of Milan, but I have already become indolent in this demoralizing clime."

Sardinia. Mayo reached the river Po and crossed into Sardinia. He is less than impressed with what his sees. "Soon after reaching the dirty river Po, the bridge of boats had just been carried away by a freshet. The passengers are detained in this miserable little village twenty-four hours. These dogs of Italians are a patient people. I am all anxiety to get over this muddy rapid, but as soon as the natives find that they have to remain for the water to subside, they go to singing and dancing as if they had met here for that purpose. I have taken refuge in the village church where I read the guide and make notes." The carriage finally crossed the river and they traveled to Genoa.

Genoa. "We descended the south side of the Apennines and entered Genoa. There are three American ships in the harbor, but where is it that this flag does not wave? The English here are said to be very jealous of the Americans, who do nearly the whole spice trade of the Mediterranean. Went to the American Hotel to procure lodgings, but the whole of it was taken by Lady Byron. Conversed with her Ladyship in the hotel without knowing that it was the once wife of Lord Byron. She has a melancholy air. Her person is good; she appears to have been rather handsome. Her daughter, Adda, is about twelve years of age and is a sweet girl."

Mayo does sightseeing in Genoa. He observes that many of the private dwellings may be called palaces, obscurely situated on very narrow streets. He thought the churches were not as splendid and paintings less numerous than in other cities. Mayo was not impressed with the appearance of the people. "The lower order of people are very homely and many of them deformed; the opulent are handsome, but the females are seldom seen. It is a matter of astonishment to me how any people can be handsome or even good looking under any monarchy, and more particularly, these pretty ones. Everyone is in continual apprehension and dread. We do not know how happy we are. We have no tyrants, either great or small, to deal with in the United States.

"Attended a ball given by an English gentleman. His youngest sister is handsome and not at all deficient. Mrs. Barry and one or two others were fine looking and intelligent women, but out of twenty-five ladies, the majority looked very, I may say, common. There were some Italian officers very polite and genteel. The rest of the company were made up of Englishmen who, of course, spoke and acted English."

Monaco and South France. On Christmas day, Mayo departed Genoa and on the 29th arrived "in the dominions of that rascal the Prince of Monaco." He then passed through Villafrance and Nice. In Nice Mayo learned that his ship the *North Carolina* was in Toulon. He rushed to take a carriage to meet his ship writing, "I am again in France but have not yet been able to decide which people I like best, the French or Italians. The country of the latter, I prefer decidedly." He writes about Antibes, "There is a monument here erected by Louis the 18th to the people of this city for their fidelity in not opening their gates to Napoleon--for which I have a most contemptible opinion; yet I am compelled to remain here twenty-four hours." On the last day of December, 1826, Mayo arrived at Toulon only to find that his ship had sailed a few days before.

Mayo spent a few days looking over the French ships in the dockyard. He writes, "The yard is kept in high order; it has every convenience necessary. The model office is well-supplied with all the models necessary in ship building, sailing, etc. The rope walk is a thousand feet long, the ship houses, store houses and all the buildings are well constructed and made to last for centuries. Went on board the *Royal Louis*, a

3-decker, mounting 130 guns. She was launched about the year 1810. She has never been to sea and never will, for she is now falling to pieces. Went on board the *Hero*, a three decker of 120 guns. She is a good model, the workmanship is very rough. Went on board the *Provina*, fitting out. The French naval force here is great and they continue to build very fast. Remained one hour in the dock yard, where they are at work upon a frigate."

The next stop in France was Marseilles. Mayo observed that, "The American merchants here are highly respected. The commercial importance of every foreign nation is soon discovered in the maritime ports of Europe. Here they have Hotel Washington, Hotel Franklin, Caffee Washington, Caffee United States, but no Caffee Great Britain." He spent two days there getting a passport to Spain, then traveled by carriage toward Barcelona. His carriage was now traversing the road from which he left Barcelona, called "double banking." One of the passengers was a lady who spoke French, Spanish, Italian, Portuguese and a little English. He wrote that, "She is an astonishing woman. She is going a distance of five hundred miles alone to see a sick father."

Return to Spain. As he left France, Mayo wrote, "Adieu to France with all her glory and all her Jesuits. Notwithstanding the wretched situation of Spain and the danger of traveling in it at present, yet I rejoice to get back to it. I think the Spaniards are before either the French or Italians in sincerity, which, by the bye, is a rare commodity in all old countries." Mayo arrived at Barcelona and looked for passage to Minorca, where he expected to find his ship, *North Carolina*. The local consul, Mr. Sterling, told him that the last vessel for Minorca had sailed three days ago and no vessel had arrived from that island for a month. Mayo had decided to take passage in a small boat, but the consul convinced him to wait a few days as a packet should soon arrive from Minorca.

Isaac Mayo remained in Barcelona. He observed, "When the day of retribution comes, for come it must, what mercy can the Jesuits and those attached to them expect. They take every means in their power to wound and torment the men who had the courage to stand forth in the defense of their degraded country. What has the Society of the Exterminating Angels at that day to expect but an extermination of its own merciless sect? This is the time of the carnival and everybody is gay. Attended the masquerades regularly where there is every species of demoralization. One may flatter or mortify and torment whom he pleases with impunity, for the guards are always ready to quiet the least disturbance. A Spaniard will always give his last paseta to visit a bull fight.

"On February 9th a severe gale from the southeast has driven most of the shipping in the harbor on shore, sinking some, and rendering many unseaworthy. Received intelligence that the boat in which I was upon the eve of embarking for the Island of Majorca has been lost and every soul on board perished. I am thankful for this escape. On the 15th set out in the Majorca Packet, but the Captain feared the weather and returned to Barcelona."

He wrote his observations of the Italians at opera as follows, " The Italians frequently go to the opera as much to play at cards, converse or sleep, as to listen to the performance. It is not uncommon to see a lounging Prince or a Duke open his eyes at some particular part and cry out, 'Bravo, Bravo' and the ladies put by their cards for a moment and sing out, 'Bravisimo, Bravisimo' to something that is very superior. They then take up cards without once again looking at the stage during the whole performance. This is considered true taste and refinement."

On February 17, 1827, Mayo embarked on the packet and thirty-six hours later he was put ashore at Mahon. The *Constitution* was in port, but *North Carolina* had been forced into Malta by bad weather. On the 27th the *North Carolina* arrived and Mayo "repaired aboard." Imagine the stories that he had to tell his shipmates about his European travels.

5
West India Squadron
1830 - 1831

"Lieutenant Mayo is a vigilant
and meritorious officer."
Commodore Elliot to the
Secretary of the Navy, 1831

The purpose of the West India Squadron was to suppress piracy against U. S. merchant shipping in the West Indies
waters. Piracy in those waters had been a problem during the
entire 17th and 18th centuries. Factors that encouraged piracy included the rich cargoes, the dense growth of mangroves
at the water's edge, making concealment and escape easy, and
the many small, uninhabited islands with secluded harbors and
passages making pirate hideouts inaccessible to vessels of any
size. No concerted, sizable effort by the U. S. Navy was made
to combat piracy in those waters until the early 1820s. At that
time Captain James Biddle was given command of a squadron
consisting of the *Macedonian, Congress, John Adams, Cyane,
Hornet, Peacock, Spark, Enterprise, Alligator, Grampus,
Shark, Porpoise* and two gunboats. The center of the pirate
activity was first Cuba and then Puerto Rico, and those countries did little to discourage it. Much of the Navy work was

done in small boats absent from the parent ships for days at a time, searching in lagoons for pirates. The worst hazard was not the pirates, but rather infection with yellow fever. There were times when it seemed the Navy vessels would be driven out of the area by yellow fever.

Biddle's flagship, *Macedonian*, had to return to Norfolk in July, 1821, after losing nearly one-third of the crew, 101 men and officers, to yellow fever. The conditions aboard ship were probably atrocious with so many delirious, vomiting men confined to the small quarters. Biddle blamed the Charlestown Naval Yard for not properly cleaning the bilges before the ship left. Newspapers tended to blame Biddle for staying so long along the Cuban coast after the sickness became evident in the season of the year that it was prevalent.[1] It was known that going to sea away from land masses reduced the sickness, but it would be 75 years before it was understood that yellow fever was spread by mosquitoes. During Mayo's tour to the area, Navy ships did not operate in the West Indies area during the summer months, but the disease was still a major problem.

A new era opened in the war against the pirates in 1823 when David Porter relieved Biddle as Commodore, and Congress appropriated half a million dollars for pirate suppression. Porter purchased and armed eight small Chesapeake Bay schooners, which he called the "Mosquito Fleet," to operate in shoal water. This "fleet" proved to be very effective. A court of inquiry report described the conditions at this time: "A large portion of the officers and men was employed in the small schooners and in open boats--in a severe climate--exposed to the heat of a tropical sun by day and to the not less dangerous dews and exhalations at night. The vessels themselves, from their size, were destitute of suitable accommodations, and the operations in which they were engaged necessarily imposed incessant fatigue and constant exposure.......It is evident that one officer was employed for sixty-eight successive days in an open barge on the north-west of Cuba, in the examination of the inlets, bays, keys, and other places of piratical resort."[2]

There are many written stories about the pirates and their battles with the Navy. No quarter was given by either side. Many accounts tell of complete annihilation of pirate groups. One such story was told by Lt. Watson, commanding *USS Seagull* with barges *Gallinipper* and *Mosquito*: "They engaged us without colors of any description, having hauled down the Spanish flag after firing the first gun. The pirates tried to escape ashore, but very few succeeded....so exasperated were our men that it was impossible for their officers to restrain them and many were killed after orders were given to grant quarters. Twenty-seven dead were counted, some sunk, five taken prisoners by the barge-men and eight taken by a party of Spaniards ashore; the officers calculated that from thirty to thirty-five were killed. The pirate schooner....was commanded by Little Devil or Diableto."[3] This event occurred in the early days of fighting pirates in the West Indies, well before Isaac Mayo arrived on the scene. However, there was the potential that such fighting could break out at any time.

One author has investigated the size of the piracy problem by reviewing records of the Marblehead Marine Insurance Co. He estimated that 500 vessels were seized by pirates with a value of the property destroyed by them at $20 million dollars. By way of comparison, the value of the property destroyed by pirates rivaled the annual cost of running the United States government in 1821 ($19,785,000, including interest and redemption of part of the public debt). An estimated two thousand pirates were actively engaged during the period of 1820-1830. Opposing them, several countries' navies captured pirate ships and crews: United States, 79 vessels, 62 guns, and 1300 men; British, 18 vessels, 20 guns and 291 men; Spanish, 5 vessels and 150 men. By far, the major burden fell on the United States to fight this war.[4]

Over the next few years, the Navy reduced piracy considerably during the winter months, but after the Navy vessels left the area in the summer to avoid the yellow fever, it would resume. Cuba cooperated to suppress piracy, but Puerto Rico did not. Finally, by 1825 there were only a few sporadic cases of piracy each year. In 1829 there was a flare-up of pirating resulting in pleas from merchants in Boston to the Secretary of the Navy; however, it seemed to be in control. The Navy relocated the headquarters of the West India Squadron from Key West to Pensacola.[5] By January, 1831, Commodore Elliot proposed that they leave Pensacola in August and September and go to Norfolk He argued that they could do nothing because of the yellow fever that plagued the ship's personnel and that commerce was at a low ebb during that period. In addition, he pointed out that ship's personnel that were discharged in Pensacola left the service, but in Norfolk they tended to reship. Elliot's proposal was not approved, and they remained in Pensacola.[6]

. On February 13, 1830, Mayo was ordered to proceed to New York City and to report for passage in *Brandywine* to the West Indies; upon arrival, he was to report to Commodore Elliot for command of the schooner *Grampus*. Lieutenant Mayo took command of the *Grampus* on April 17, 1830, after traveling aboard *Brandywine* to Havana where the squadron was located.

By the time Isaac Mayo was assigned to the Squadron in 1830, it was primarily convoying merchant vessels, investigating various reports of potential piracy and maintaining a naval presence in the area.[7]

One trick that the Squadron sought to prevent was employed by some American merceant vessels to avoid payment of Spanish duties in Havana and United States duties while in our ports. Ships loaded with American goods would hoist a Spanish flag before entry into Havana to avoid duties there, and on the return, carrying Spanish goods, they would hoist a flag of the United States upon entering our ports As such episodes were reported by the Havana authorities, the U.S. Squadron would respond to investigate. It is not apparent that this practice was aggressively pursued; only Havana complaints were investigated.[8]

During this period a revolution took place in Colombia which endangered our shipping to those ports. Squadron ships were periodically sent to show the flag in the various ports and to demonstrate a U.S. naval presence in those waters. In addition, a few Colombian vessels engaged in piracy and were hunted, with the objective of capturing them and sending them to New York City. In one such "hunting" trip to Colombia, the Commanding Officer was directed as follows, "should it be in your power, within the range of your Cruise to add to improvement of the growth of the sugar cane of our Country , you will not omit doing so, by having samples conveyed to the United States necessary for this purpose." Apparently, someone in Washington was able to require the Secretary of the Navy to do a little commercial spying for them.[9]

In May, 1830, the crew of the *Grampus* was found to be suffering from a skin disease. It was incapacitating men for duty and had a "tendency to cast a gloom over their spirits." Mayo concluded that it was caused by the use of salt provisions in the climate, based on the observation that the men recovered once they had fresh fish and vegetables. Thereafter, he sought to find fresh provisions at every opportunity.[10]

The Master of the brig, *Kremlin*, of Boston reported an incident with a pirate ship in early June, 1830, in which the *Grampus* arrived just in time to save him. He wrote that off the Island of Santa Domingo, at daylight, a suspicious schooner appeared and followed him for almost a day. His letter reported, "Ultimately the ship approach within speaking distance and showing every symptom of hostility, his men being at a long mounted gun amidships. I called all hands and cleared away my three guns for action, distributing my small arms among my crew, being under the firm conviction that his intention was to attack me. He peremptorily ordered me to send my boat on board; I observed to him that my boat leaked and could not send her. He had, all the while, shown no colors It is my positive belief that nothing but my show of resistance prevented his attacking me. He then said he would send his boat to me; my vessel is high-sided and I did not shorten sail for him. He ultimately hoisted Spanish colors, crossed my bow and luffed off, then he jibed and stood again towards me. At this moment I discovered a vessel standing for me which soon after was spoken as the U.S. schooner *Grampus*."[11] The pirate ship turned out to be the *Phenix*. Mayo captured *Phenix*, kept its crew aboard *Grampus*, and sent it to New Orleans with a prize crew. He noted in his private journal that it was sold there "for the benefit of the captor." The captors were Mayo and the crew of *Grampus*.

In September, 1830, an episode indicating the health conditions on the ships of the Squadron was reported. The *Peacock* was completely disabled by the combination of the yellow fever and the availability of alcohol in Pensacola. The Commodore reported, "I apprised you of the measures taken towards the restoration of the health of the Officers and Crew with the momentary purity of the air onboard the *Peacock*. I regret extremely to say that further indisposition has presented itself arising from the debaucherous habits of the seamen, exposure to the disease, and then indulgence in the use of ardent spirits, conveyed clandestinely to them from Pensacola. Obviously the Marine Guard proving defective, I have employed guards from the town." This wasn't the only problem the Commodore had with the Marine Corps. He had an officer ordered to his staff who refused to board ship, but rather stayed in Pensacola. He was under orders from the Commandant of the Marine Corps and did not report to the Commodore; such confusion was corrected in later years.[12]

A flurry of activity for the Squadron followed in January, 1831, when a group of pirates led by Antonio Marino, alias La Tonta, escaped from a Havana fort. They were reported to have taken a small sloop and were cruising east of Cuba, "committing depredations." The Squadron searched for them without success. The Cuban Navy did find them and shot La Tonta. At this same time, signs of revolution in Cuba greatly worried the U. S. merchants in the area. The Squadron responded by convoying U.S. merchant ships until the danger died down.[13]

On March 3, 1831, the *Grampus* went aground at the entrance to the port of Havana. Mayo reported that a sudden gust of wind from the land struck the mainsail, leaving the head sails flapping, which broached the ship to the ground. She was soon gotten off and without any apparent injury, with the exception of losing a fluke of one of the anchors in housing it.[14] Grounding was not a career-ending event in those days. Poor charts and the uncertainty of the weather effects on the sailing ships made grounding a fairly common experience. For example, in January, 1831, the *Natchez* had run aground at Key West on a coral reef while trying to enter the harbor without a pilot. That same ship had run aground at the Cayman Passage about four months earlier. Apparently, the copper on the bottom of the *Natchez* was severely damaged and in need of replacement before summer to avoid worm damage to the underlying wood.[15] There also was an incident during this period in which the flagship, *Erie*, ran aground.

Isaac Mayo informed the Commodore on March 6, 1831, that he had applied to be relieved from the command of the *Grampus*. The Commodore wrote to the Secretary of the Navy that Mayo "is a vigilant and meritorious officer and if it accords with the views of the Department, I hope he may be indulged." The Commodore asked that he be permitted to replace Mayo with one of the Lieutenants in the Squadron because "they who are daily exposed to the danger of cruising in an unhealthy station, should possess some claims to share any incidental honors or advantages which may present themselves." Mayo was relieved on April 20, 1831, by Lieutenant Tattnall.[16]

Lieutenant Tattnall was required to inspect the *Grampus* shortly afterwards. He reported that it was in deplorable condition. He found all of the copper off the bow and the copper on the forefoot very much damaged, due to the grounding in Havana harbor. Her battery also was such that all the gun screws were out of order and the locks totally useless. The boats were in a "very ruinous condition," and the only navigating instrument on board was a sextant that could be used only in the day with great difficulty and could not be used at night at all.[17] It appears that Mayo had decided to live with the ship's poor material condition, perhaps because complaining to your Commodore was not a very career-enhancing move.

On December 20, 1832, Isaac Mayo was promoted to Master Commandant. He remained on leave until 1837 when he took command of the *Fairfield* in the Brazil Squadron.

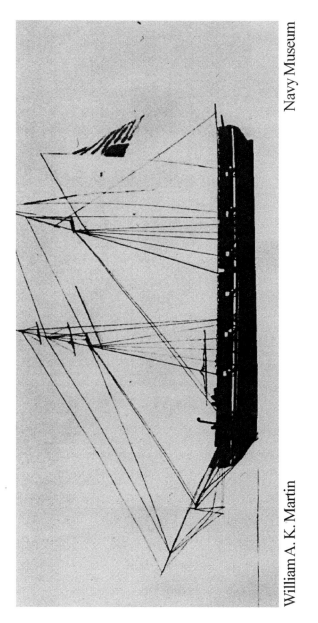

William A. K. Martin

Navy Museum

USS GRAMPAS - COMMANDED BY MAYO IN WEST INDIES, 1830-31

6
Brazil Squadron
1837-1838

*"Our Commander, Isaac Mayo....was
a brave and skillful officer,
courteous to all under his command."*
Solomon H. Sanborn, former crew
member, *USS Fairfield,* 1841.

Master Commandant Isaac Mayo had been promoted
to that rank in 1832 and had been ashore without an assignment from 1831 to 1837. During that time he had started to
assemble his properties in the area between the Rhode and
South Rivers in Anne Arundel County (he owned 500 acres
by this time). In 1835 he married Sarah Bland, daughter of
Theodoric Bland, Chancellor of Maryland, and their first
daughter, Sarah, was born in 1836. In 1837 Mayo was assigned to command the eighteen-gun sloop of war, *USS
Fairfield,* to serve in Brazil in a squadron protecting American shipping from piracy. Isaac Mayo reported to his ship in
March, 1837, in Norfolk (the naval base was called Gosport
at that time) and departed Norfolk for Brazil on April 25, 1837.
The crew was assembled from personnel at the base, from the
USS Java and from the *USS Porpoise.* Just before the ship

79

left, Mayo wrote a letter about the inexperience of his crew. He said that "when the topsman are aloft there are not ten men on deck that know one rope from another, as was evinced in coming from the Navy Yard to the anchorage." There was no gunner, only one-forth of the seamen allowed and 45 landsmen (no experience at all).[1] Because of the prevailing winds, the *Fairfield* proceeded first to Cape Verde Islands (Port Praya). There, the Vice Consul asked Mayo to look into the situation on the schooner *Fanny Butler* whose papers were irregular. Mayo found out that all of the vessels engaged in the slave trade flew American colors so that the patrols of British and Portuguese vessels would not interfere. He recommended to the Secretary of the Navy that the U.S. place vessels in the area to prevent American ships from engaging in the slave trade.[2] This was done many years later.

Mayo arrived in Rio de Janeiro on July 2, 1837, delivering a dispatch that sent the current flagship, *USS Erie*, and the Commodore home. The new Commodore was to be John B. Nicholson in the flagship, *USS Independence*. Since the new Commodore would be some time en route, Isaac Mayo became the Senior Officer, Brazil Squadron, with the brig, *USS Dolphin*, under his command.[3] In August he ordered the *Dolphin* to go to Montevideo to assess the political situation there. Its commander reported back that there were states of revolution in Peru, Uruguay, Argentina and Chile, based on reports from American residents and merchants in the area, but that all Americans felt safe.[4]

In mid-August Mayo reported to the Secretary of the Navy that the situation in the Brazilian Province of Rio Grande (located at the southern end of Brazil on the coast) continued to deteriorate as the result of the revolution there. Apparently the American Consul to that Province was imprisoned, and American merchants had to suspend their commercial operations. Mayo

wrote that, "As far as I can learn, all the outrages have been committed by the Imperial or Brazilian Government, as they take it for
granted that every citizen of the United States is on the side of the
Patriots or as they call them the Insurgents, but have in no case
produced proof of interference. I am called upon most urgently
by our countrymen residing in Brazil as well as by presentations of
those living in Buenos Aires to visit Rio Grande for their protection. I shall attempt to get *Dolphin* over the bar and I shall cruise
off the bar in *Fairfield* as long as may be necessary."[5]

In mid-October Mayo reported an outbreak of smallpox
on *Dolphin*. He had experience with smallpox on the *USS North
Carolina* when he was aboard her in the Mediterranean in 1827,
so he knew what had to be done. Mayo landed the sick on an
island, sending officers to maintain discipline and cleanliness. Then
they fumigated *Dolphin* for several days in succession; every part
of the ship was broken out and ventilated. The *Dolphin* was to
remain at the island (near Rio Grande) and not return to Rio de
Janeiro until all smallpox was cleared up.[6] This evidently took
about a month. Interestingly, at the end of October, Mayo sent a
letter to the Secretary of the Navy requesting that he be relieved
of duty in *Fairfield* in April, 1838, so that he could attend to
personal affairs at home. He had been appointed executor of his
sister's estate which amounted to $30,000.[7]

The *USS Independence* was required to deliver
a consul to St. Petersburg before coming to Brazil, and didn't
arrive in the area until November 20, 1837. When Commodore
Nicholson arrived in Bahia, he found a state of revolution existed.
He told the Secretary of the Navy that his arrival offered protection to Americans and Europeans in the area who feared for their
lives. Nicholson requested two more sloops to provide protection for American interests in Brazil. Meanwhile the *Fairfield*

and *Dolphin* were in Rio de Janeiro near the seat of the Brazilian Government. The *Fairfield* proceeded to Bahia and Mayo met with the new Commodore on November 25, 1837.[8]

Some background in the history of Brazil is needed to appreciate what was happening in Bahia where Mayo and his ship spent most of their time after the arrival of the Commodore. The *USS Independence* could usually be found in Rio de Janeiro. Brazil, of course, started as a Portuguese colony. In the time of Napoleon (early 1800s) Portugal was captured by the French, the Portuguese Royal family moved to Brazil, and the British assumed the protection of Brazil. Of course, the British were very interested in exploiting the commercial aspects of the arrangement and moved aggressively to do so. By 1837 the Brazilian government was run by the Regency, a group of Brazilian politicians who were to be an interim government until the young Dom Pedro II became old enough to govern.

During this period various rebellions broke out in different parts of Brazil. The one involving Isaac Mayo occurred in Bahia. Called the Sabinada Revolt; it lasted from 1837 to 1838. The seaport for the province of Bahia was Salvador, and the revolt was confined to that city. The Sabinada Revolt got its name from its principal leader, Sabino Barroso, a newspaperman and professor in Bahia's medical school. Bahia had been the scene of several urban revolts, including slave revolts. The Sabinada gathered wide support, which included Salvador's middle and merchant classes. It espoused federalist and republican ideas. The planters outside Salvador did not support the revolt; rather, they supported the government. After besieging Salvador by land and sea, government forces took the city in hand-to-hand fighting which left nearly 1,800 people dead.[9]

In late November, 1837, Commodore Nicholson received a request from the President of Bahia that the United States loan arms to the Government since all of their arms had been taken by the Revolutionary forces in Salvador. The Commodore denied the request, explaining that he had been instructed to maintain strict neutrality between the forces.[10]

Mayo became involved in a dispute with the local Bahia Government in late December, 1837. The Bahia President had established a new place to collect duties on an island in the Salvador Bay since the city itself was held by Revolutionary forces. The President had not informed foreign countries, but had instructed his ships to enforce the new duty collection site. Apparently, a Brazilian Navy ship fired two shots at an American merchant ship with the intent to direct it to the island and collect duties, even though it had not discharged any cargo. Mayo observed the shots, got his ship underway and cleared the decks for battle. The Brazilian Commander boarded the *Fairfield* to discuss the situation. He later complained that he was treated disrespectfully by Mayo, that the *USS Fairfield* showed its guns to him and that it had cleared its decks for action. Mayo, in his reply to the American Consul, pointed out that his guns were mounted and that they always showed. Further, he had not been disrespectful--the complaint that he kept the Brazilian standing in his stateroom on the *Fairfield* was the result of having prepared the ship for battle; there simply was no place to sit. He pointed out that any naval commander would prepare for action when meeting a foreign ship under such circumstances.[11]

The situation continued to deteriorate with conflicting positions between the President of Bahia and his Government in Rio de Janeiro concerning whether the port of Salvador was under blockade. Mayo observed that it was under blockade for American ships but not for British ships, and reported to his Commodore that the blockade was illegal. His Commodore completely supported his position. About this time, the U.S. Charge d'Affairs in Rio wrote to the Commodore that he had been to a meeting with the Brazilian Foreign Secretary, who had specifically complained about Mayo. The Charge d'Affairs said that Mayo was substantially right, but that "there is a feeling against him and if it be true that the insurrection President dined on board his ship by his invitation, it is enough to excite the indictment of this jealous people." In this same letter the U.S. Charge d'Affairs asked that Mayo be relieved of his command "to save us from difficulty."[12] The Commodore decided the best thing to do was to get Mayo out of the harbor and to replace the *Fairfield* with the *Dolphin*. This was ordered in mid-January, 1838, subject to Mayo's evaluation of the situation. In the same letter he cautioned Mayo not to write letters to the President or any other official, but rather to discuss matters face-to-face, to assure no misunderstandings.[13] The Commodore wrote to the Charge d'Affairs that Mayo could not be relieved and that, as far as he was concerned, many of the charges were just rumors. His information indicated that Mayo had acted properly to protect the U.S. rights as neutrals, and that he had done no more than a commander should do to protect the rights of his fellow citizens. He also stated that an investigation to ascertain the facts would be necessary to relieve Mayo, and the Secretary of the Navy would have to approve it.[14]

Having decided that he should not leave Bahia, Mayo wrote to the Commodore on February sixth that a decisive battle would occur soon. In that letter he also described several small naval skirmishes between the government and the revolutionaries in the Bahia harbor. He added that he planned to leave Bahia in 2 to 3 days.[15] This decision seems surprising, since the Commodore had made it clear that he wanted Mayo out of Bahia, saying in his letter, "return to this port without delay. Should you not suppose it necessary in consequence of occurrences there of which I must have you to be the judge, ...send *Dolphin* with your dispatches announcing to me the necessity of your remaining. I however hope this will not be the case and I shall have the pleasure of seeing you here as soon as wind and weather will permit." *Fairfield* departed Bahia on February eleventh and arrived at Rio on February nineteenth. By then Mayo was satisfied that conditions in Bahia were stable and that ships of all nations were receiving equal treatment. On February twenty-fourth, 1838, Commodore Nicholson reported to the Secretary of the Navy that the Brazilian Government had withdrawn their previous letters concerning Mayo, based on the conclusion that the information upon which they were based had proven incorrect, and that Mayo had only performed his duty. The Commodore reported that "everything is upon the most friendly position between the Imperial Government here and ourselves."[16]

Isaac Mayo received permission from the Secretary of the Navy to leave *Fairfield* on August 30, 1838. His Commodore was extremely unhappy with Mayo's departure before the cruise was over and told the Secretary of the Navy exactly what he thought. Some of his thoughts were, "Change of command on station leads to much expense and more than this, it is disruptive of discipline and leads to insubordination as but few have the same opinions on this important subject and thus the crew become dissatisfied when they see their officers desert them and new officers lead them. To have a ship effective the officers and crew should know each other and remain together if possible."[17] Mayo reached the U.S. in early November and was granted leave to attend to his personal business.

This tour of duty in Brazil demonstrated Mayo's strong sense of duty to his nation and his willingness to take professional risks to see that the job was done to his standards. He was quick to recognize and take action when United States merchant ships were threatened or received unequal treatment. He refused to leave his station, even though his Commodore clearly wanted him out of Bahia, until he was satisfied that the situation was normalized. The scurious attacks by the Brazilian Government on his reputation apparently had no effect on his actions, a difficult and courageous act on his part.

.

Navy Museum

USS FAIRFIELD-COMMANDED BY MAYO IN BRAZIL, 1837-38

Nav W. Secretary   _January 22 - 1837_
of the Navy

     Sir

       When the officers are ordered to the Hartford, you will oblige me by allowing Midn. [G.] R. P. Rodgers to one of the Midshipmen to be attached to said ship

       I have the honor to be
       Sir most respectfully
       your Obt. Servt.
       Isaac Mayo
       Master Commandt.

Hon W. M. Dickerson
Secy. of the Navy

Archives of the U. S, Navy Department

LETTER FROM ISAAC MAYO TO THE SECRETARY OF THE NAVY, JANUARY 22, 1837

7

Second Seminole War 1839

"When freedom from her mountain height
Unfurled her standard to the air
She tore the azure robe of night
And set her stars of glory there."
'The American Flag'--Percival
Isaac Mayo's Journal

Commander Mayo served as Commanding Officer of the steamer, *Poinsett*, during part of the Second Seminole War in Florida in 1839-1840. Isaac Mayo apparently felt that this service was noteworthy because he made specific mention of it in a summary of service that he prepared. In it he wrote, "Ordered to the Steamer *Poinsett* as Comdr. with a Squadron of Gun Boats in the Seminole War; captured 'Mad Tiger' and ten Indian warriors."[1] Histories of the Seminole War do not mention Mayo's role in the war, nor do they acknowledge that the Navy had any part in the conflict. In fact, the effort put forth by Mayo and his Navy force was a very minor part of the long, difficult war waged against the Seminoles by the United States. Recent authors interested in riverine warfare have renewed interest in the Second Seminole War because it was an early example of that difficult type of war.

Florida belonged to Spain until 1822. A serious problem arose when slaves from the southern United States escaped to Florida, and took refuge with the Seminole Indians, who would not willingly return them. The First Seminole War came in 1817-1818 when Andrew Jackson occupied much of Florida, burned Indian villages and executed two British citizens. Shortly thereafter Spain ceded Florida to the United States. Turmoil continued, so the government decided to move the Indians to the western United States. The Second Seminole War started in 1835 when the moves to the West were begun. The war was primarily a war of attrition; by 1839 about three-fourths of the Seminoles had left the area, and those remaining had withdrawn to the Everglades in South Florida. The fighting was then waged by Indians using guerrilla tactics. The Army realized that help from the Navy would be required to maintain communications around the perimeter of the Everglades and to penetrate the swamp.[2]

In 1835 the U. S. Navy was very small: 785 officers and 3,627 sailors, augmented by 58 officers and 1,177 men in the Marine Corps. The Navy had eighteen ships organized into five squadrons. One of the squadrons was the West India, consisting of one frigate, two sloops-of-war, and a schooner. The West India Squadron's primary responsibility was protection of merchant shipping from piracy. In the years 1835 to 1839 most of the Naval effort in Florida was concentrated on blockading the Seminoles to prevent their receiving guns and munitions from Cuba.

During this period there were several expeditions into the Everglades using small boats manned by sailors and marines, led by Lt. Levin M. Powell, USN, with varying degrees of success. The Seminoles proved to be superb guerrilla fighters. These operations were often joint actions, employing tactics using small boats and combined operations with the Army in a search and destroy effort in the Everglades. In addition to the blockade and the swamp penetration effort, the Navy also had the task of protecting shipwrecked crews from attacks by the Seminoles. Many episodes of ship wrecks on the coast of South Florida occurred and almost always the survivors were attacked by Indians with severe losses inflicted by the Seminoles. Thus, during this period there were three naval operating forces around Florida with diverse tasks and vessels without a unifying command. Each acted independently, reacting mainly to Indian episodes.[3]

In 1839 the Navy modified its command structure in Florida, no longer requiring the West India Squadron to assist the Army in Florida. On April 5, 1839, the Secretary of the Navy placed Commander Isaac Mayo in charge of the Expedition for the Suppression of Indian Hostilities, Florida. His force, nonetheless, remained under the operational control of the War Department (Army). Mayo's command consisted of the steamer *Poinsett*, the schooner *Wave* and several barges.[4] (The *Wave*, with its Commanding Officer, Lt. McLaughlin, returned to the North before Mayo arrived because the enlistment terms of a large part of the crew were about to end.) Mayo was ordered to Baltimore to inspect the *Fulton* and to acquire information concerning the management of steam engines and machinery before he departed for Florida.[5] The West India Squadron Commodore was ordered, "As this is considered by the Department as special service, distinct from any connected with your Command, you will not interfere in any manner with his (Mayo's) operations."[6] As a result of this directive, Isaac Mayo asked the Secretary of the Navy to give him permission to hoist the flag of a squadron commander, but the Secretary refused, saying that Mayo's force and mission were not considered sufficient to warrant that distinction.[7]

The *Poinsett* had been purchased by the Army in August, 1837, having been called the *New Brighton* before the Army acquired her. She had both sails and side paddle-wheels; was 133 feet long with a beam of 22 feet, depth of hold of 9 feet and a draft of 6 feet. *Poinsett* carried a long thirty-two pounder pivot gun and had a speed of eight knots. The engines were fueled by wood.[8] The need for wood fuel was a major disadvantage for the *Poinsett*. It took several days to gather fuel sufficient for one day's travel, so the range of the ship was limited. On the Florida east coast there were no harbors between St. Augustine and Key Biscayne to provide shelter from storms, and therefore the *Poinsett* was not well adapted for such service. When Mayo first arrived in Florida, he proposed that small, shallow-draft, steam-driven craft be used to fight the Seminoles. He thought that two of such, about 35 feet long, and drawing no more than twelve inches of water, with a crew of thirty and a capability of carrying a month's supply of provisions, would be ideal. He suggested that rifle-proof sections, three to five feet high, with loopholes, should be installed around the sides in such a manner that they could be placed and removed from the rail. The main armament would be a four or six-pounder similarly protected, firing through a porthole. Such a vessel would be essentially a floating fort; Mayo felt it would be futile to attempt to penetrate the Everglades in open boats with the crew exposed to gunfire from dense underbush.[9] At that time he did not realize that the Seminoles simply appeared and disappeared and the warfare that he envisioned, battles of groups of men using cannon, was not to be. He also learned, as he gained experience, that the steamer boat was too wasteful of manpower to use in the swamp environment because of the large effort required to collect wood fuel.

Commodore Mayo's trip to Florida turned out to be more eventful than he expected. When Mayo left Baltimore in early June, 1839, he decided to tow two of the four gunbarges assigned to the *Poinsett* to determine the practicability of taking them to Florida in this manner. By the time he reached Norfolk he realized the great danger to the boats from any strong wind, and he requested transportation for those barges which could not be carried aboard the steamer. Soon after Mayo left Norfolk on June 26, he ran into a heavy wind from the south just after rounding Cape Hatteras. He tried to make it to Ocracoke Inlet, North Carolina, before his fuel supply was depleted, but headwinds made this impossible.

The *Poinsett* then sprang a leak, forcing him to turn away from the storm to minimize taking on water. He turned northward, running with the storm until it abated. By this time he did not have enough fuel to make any ports to the south and he was even compelled to burn some of the ship's superstructure in order to reach Cape Henry, where he met the steamer *South Carolina* and received enough wood to return to Norfolk. He departed again on July 3, arriving three days later at Charleston, South Carolina, and finally reaching Garey's Ferry, Florida, (on the St. Johns River) on July 12.[10]

Mayo decided to use Key Biscayne as his base of operations and from there distribute his barges along the keys as far as Key West or the Dry Tortugas. On the way to Key Biscayne he stopped at St Augustine where the local paper reported: "The *Poinsett*, painted black, with her white painted ports, looks about the guards as gay as a sloop of war, and above has as much top hamper as a load of hay. She draws six feet of water, and though schooner rigged, will run a chance of getting snagged on the reefs if a pretty considerable supply of wood is not in readiness. What with a small vessel, red hot boilers, a vertical sun, smoke, cinders and mangrove-key mosquitoes, the officers and crew may anticipate delightful cruising."[11]

After gathering wood for his vessel at Key Biscayne, Mayo organized a small force to explore the Everglades in that area. When they returned to *Poinsett*, Mayo found Chief Mad Tiger (Catsha Tustenuggee) with twenty Indians visiting aboard the steamer. The Commander ordered his wood and water parties to proceed well-armed and to exercise care after that visit. Just after Mad Tiger and his group had departed *Poinsett*, Mayo received notification that an Army command under Colonel Harney, fifteen miles up the Caloosahatchee River, had been attacked on July 23, 1839, by war parties from Hospetarke's and Chakaika's bands. Thirteen of the twenty-six man detachment were killed; Colonel Harney and the other thirteen men escaped. Taking no chances, Mayo immediately ordered a landing party assembled and the cutters launched. He departed in his gig to overtake one of the canoes and did so after a three hour row. He captured a group of Indians, as did two other officers, one using a cutter and the other using the ship's dingy. Mayo then set out after Chief Mad Tiger, who was across the bay. Quite a long and difficult chase ensued. Both Mad Tiger and Mayo used a combination of sails and rowing, but finally the sailors outperformed the Indians and caught Mad Tiger. Even after being caught, the Seminole chief tried to escape to his canoe which was being towed behind; however, the sailors subdued him. Mayo turned all of the captured Indians over to Colonel Harney.[12]

Four days after the Mad Tiger episode, the *Poinsett* found a merchant ship, *Grand Turk* of Boston, beached at Fowey Rocks. Mayo's crew managed to refloat her and bring her inside the reef, but she was too damaged, and it was necessary to beach her. As soon as a salvage wrecker appeared, Mayo left the area for Key Biscayne.[13]

The transports with the barges from Norfolk arrived at Key Biscayne soon after Mayo's arrival. The barges were distributed with one remaining at Key Biscayne, one at Indian Creek and one at Key West. Mayo had a house built on Key Biscayne to store the expedition's supplies. He then proceeded up the west Florida coast to the former site of Colonel Harney's post on the Caloosahatchee. A fishing vessel had reported to him at Key West that a white flag had been seen flying over a block house near Cape Sable. Mayo thought it might be a signal from some survivors of the Colonel Harney massacre, but it was not. Up the Caloosahatchee, he found the post store and other buildings still standing, but all the contents had been plundered. After spending a few days searching this area, he steamed to Tampa to meet with General Taylor. General Taylor told Mayo that negotiations were going on with two Indian chiefs and to show no force in the area of Key Biscayne until the talks were over.[14] Mayo wrote to the Secretary of Navy that he felt that the Indians were only trying to gain time and gifts from the Army. He also surmised that the Seminoles would not leave the east coast because of the rich plunder available from wrecked ships along the shore line.[15]

Disease was a significant problem for the military forces in Florida. A severe outbreak of the fever appeared among the crew of the barge Mayo had left at Indian Key. Mayo visited the group in September, 1839, and found the officer and crew very sick. He had them evacuated to the *Poinsett*, where two of the men died within two hours. The officer also died several days later. Mayo found the camp quarters filthy, brine had escaped from salt provisions and the stench from spoiled food was overpowering. A Midshipman and some crew went ashore to clean up the camp and continue barge operations; however, in a few days the officer and some of the men became sick. Mayo then constructed a sail-loft to act as an infirmary and sent his surgeon and assistant surgeon ashore to care for the sick. Shortly thereafter, the surgeon and three attendants became sick. They recovered; then the Assistant Surgeon became sick. By the end of October all the sickness had disappeared and the infirmary was discontinued.[16]

Mayo's misgivings about the Indians' intentions were shortly confirmed. Two men at the Army garrison at Fort Lauderdale were killed when they accepted an invitation to go to a party the Indians were giving. Mayo brought his ship and all his barges to Fort Lauderdale, but the Indians did not attack. He decided to follow them into the Everglades using two gunbarges and two smaller craft. He went up the Little River, the Snake River and the Miami River but found no Indian activity. He then dispersed his force along the coast with instructions to continue to probe the Everglades for the enemy. One group was based at Fort Lauderdale, and a second group at Fort Kemble for the search and destroy activity. A third group guarded the stores at Key Biscayne with the ship's cutter, as they patrolled the coast, seeking wrecked vessels. When the force was properly positioned, the *Poinsett* went to St. Augustine.[17] There the *Poinsett* developed serious boiler trouble and had to return north for repairs. The Secretary of the Navy directed that Mayo leave his personnel and barges on the coast for use by Lt. McLaughlin, who was issued orders to proceed to Florida. Mayo returned to Washington, D.C., in December, 1839.

After his return to Washington, Mayo made a series of recommendations to the Secretary of the Navy regarding the Florida operations. He proposed that the *Poinsett* not return, instead advising reliance on the barges already on station. The barges carried tents, a week's supply of rations and had a good range along the coast. He also indicated that he had developed tactics from dealing with the Seminoles, but did not want to make them official.[18] It is not known what these tactics were, but presumably they were discussed with the Secretary of the Navy. The Secretary accepted Mayo's recommendations and implemented them.

Isaac Mayo's Florida service lasted for about six months. This tour of duty was cut short because of the condition of the *Poinsett's* boilers. The old steamers, such as the *Poinsett*, used salt water and had a very short on-station life before maintenance was required. The duty was unpleasant and dangerous, but Mayo loved a good fight. He brought an experienced, mature Naval presence to a scene badly in need of unification. The command situation, operational command by the Army and administrative command by the Navy, was fraught with potential career-ending possibilities. It was to be typical of the kind of commands he was to receive in the future; i.e., dangerous with little chance of a prestigious ending.

One author has criticized Mayo for not developing tactics to enter the Everglades and aggressively taking the battle to the Seminoles. In Mayo's defense, he was given a ship and craft unsuited for swamp warfare. His principal assistant, Lt. McLaughlin, and the *Wave* were absent during his entire time in Florida. Further, his assignment from the Secretary of the Navy was to blockade, assist shipwrecked mariners, and assist the Army. All of these things he did diligently and aggressively to the satisfaction of the Secretary of the Navy and the Army. Had he been able to stay in Florida longer, he may have developed suitable tactics for swamp fighting. He was able to maintain good relations with the Army, a characteristic that he showed again later in the Mexican War. Mayo was promoted to Captain, USN, on September 8, 1841, further evidence of his exemplary service in Florida.

A personal note about Isaac Mayo and his assignment to Florida--he named one of his daughters Sophia Florida Bland Mayo. She was born on September 19, 1839, while he was in Florida.

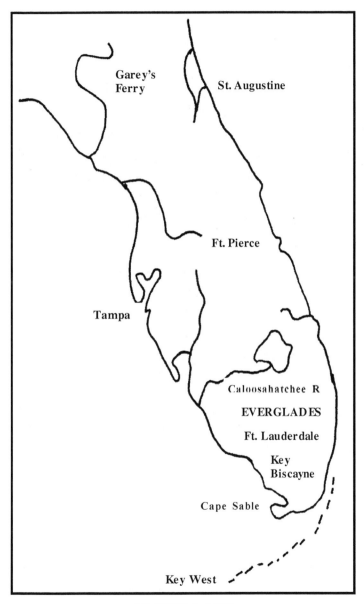

FLORIDA 1839

STEAMER POINSETT-COMMANDED BY MAYO IN FLORIDA. 1839

Courtesy Mariners' Museum

8
Africa Squadron
1843

"Stately yon vessel sails adown the tide,
To some far distant land adventurous bound.
The sailors: busy cries from side to side,
Pealing amongst the echoing rocks.
A patient, thoughtless, much enduring band,
Joyous they enter on this ocean way."
Author unknown
Isaac Mayo's Journal

The Navy established the Africa Squadron to carry out the provisions of the Webster-Ashburton Treaty of 1842 between the United States and Great Britain. The objective of the treaty was to suppress the slave trade from western Africa. Article eight of the treaty stipulated that each party would maintain a naval force of at least 80 guns on the coast of Africa to search its own nationals; that the squadrons would operate independently of each other, but would cooperate with each other in suppressing the slave trade. The Squadron operated from the years 1843 to 1861.[1] Commodore Matthew Calbraith Perry was assigned as the first squadron Commodore. He was the brother of Oliver Hazard Perry of Lake Erie fame in the War of 1812. Matthew Perry is best known as the leader of the Japan Expedition of 1853-1854.

Four ships composed that first Africa Squadron: 36-gun sloop *Macedonian* (Capt. Isaac Mayo, commanding), 22-gun sloop *Saratoga* (Capt. Josiah Tattnall, commanding), 16-gun sloop *Decatur* (Commander Joel Abbot, commanding) and the brig *Porpoise*. Mayo's officers on the *Macedonian* were John Contee, Flag Lt., Thomas C. Craven, Charles H. Poor, B. W. Hunter, J.J. Almy, William B. Whiting, James McCormick, and Matthew C. Perry, Acting Master. Matthew C. Perry was the son of the Commodore.[2] Lt. John Contee was the son of John Contee, who was a Marine 2nd Lt. aboard the *Constitution* during the War of 1812 when she defeated the British ship, *Java*, and the British ship, *Guerriere*. Both father and son were born in Prince Georges County, Maryland.[3] The senior Contee was said to have purchased the plantation, "Java," on the Rhode River with his prize money from the *Java* battle. Java was very near the Mayo property, "Gresham."

The *Saratoga* served as Commodore Perry's first flagship. He departed Sandy Hook on June 5, 1843, to rendezvous with the other three ships of the squadron in Cape Verde Islands. On September 9, 1843, the squadron met at Porto Grande, Cape Verde Islands, and Commodore Perry shifted his flag to the *Macedonian*. Apparently Perry and Tattnall did not agree on some matters. Speculation centers on the strict sanitary regulations issued by Commodore Perry as an attempt to avoid the yellow fever rampant along the African Coast. Perry learned these safeguards from the British during previous Navy duty in the area in 1820. At that time no one knew that yellow fever resulted from mosquito bites; most believed that it was spread by "noxious exhalations."

The regulations required that every man wear a flannel undershirt day and night, and turn into his hammock wearing a cloth jacket and pants. Another rule required every sailor to scrub himself clean once a week. Fresh air, supplied through the hatches from canvas windsails and encouraged to circulate by a system of fans and bellows, was dried by portable anthracite stoves between decks. Lighted smudges discouraged vermin. Finally, shore liberty terminated at 8 p.m. when regulations required all personnel to be aboard ship. Captain Mayo strictly enforced these rules, and *Macedonian* had no yellow fever or other sickness aboard during his period of command. *Saratoga*, however, became infested with sickness in this same time period.[4]

Africa Squadron orders were very specific. They stated, in part, "You are charged with the protection of American Commerce in that quarter, and with the suppression of the Slave Trade, so far as the same may be carried on by American Citizens or under the American Flag. The United States are sincerely desirous wholly to suppress the iniquitous traffic and with that view have declared it to be piracy." Squadron commanders were warned of slaver tricks such as the use of false papers, an unusual number of water casks aboard, the use of a false log book, the shipping list showing extravagant wages paid to the crew, and forged consular certificates. They were not to allow the American flag to be used for evasive or criminal purposes. Their orders required them to cruise from Madeira and the Canaries to the Bight of Biafra and from the African coast to longitude 30 degrees West. The Navy planned a depot for stores and provisions at Porto Praia (Cape Verde), and every two months a vessel would be sent there or to some other insular port for rest and replenishment.[5]

Commodore Perry also considered it his responsibility to help American colonists in Liberia by protecting them against hostile natives, although that was not in his orders from the Secretary of the Navy. Many histories concerning the slave trade and the role of the Africa Squadron criticize the small size of the squadron, the long periods they spent away from the African coast, the relatively few slavers they actually captured, and their preoccupation with commercial interests. One historian at the turn of the century said Perry's performance during this duty in Africa "should bring a blush of shame to the face of everyone who is proud of the navy's glory."[6] A later history written by the highly respected Samuel Eliot Morison, however, states that these conclusions "are completely contrary to fact."[7] The statement by Morison appears to be the more accurate.

Service in the Africa Squadron was not considered a favorable duty station. Yellow fever posed a very real threat, it was hard work and adverse criticism prevailed. There was no place to go for amusement such as would be found in other stations. There were no safe anchorages, and the paucity of fresh vegetables or fruit in this portion of Africa presented a major problem. Natives caught edible fish in the waters but refused to sell any to ships, fearing leftovers thrown in the water would frighten away the living fish. The Navy rejected the idea of establishing a supply station in the area because of concerns with the health of people who would man the station. Instead, they established the supply station on the Cape Verde Islands in Porto Praia where fresh provisions and fruit grown on the island could be obtained.[8] The distance between Porto Praia and the area of the African coast where the slave trade flourished, the limited stores that ships could carry, and the time it took for the sailing vessels to traverse the distance to and from Porto Praia presented major problems in mounting effective patrols. By 1859 the Navy had assigned steamers with coaling and supply ships to the Africa Squadron which greatly improved the effectiveness of the fleet.

The slavers did not carry heavy guns to fight the Navy; rather they depended on speed and stealth to avoid detection. Their mode of operation required them to make contacts with slave suppliers in Africa, then go off coast. At prearranged signals, the slaver would approach and receive the slaves from several small boats. The pickups were made at night. The American captain of the slaver then left the ship, transferring the vessel to others. If patrols caught the ship before the slaves were loaded, all could be "explained." For example, water casks were labeled as wine, food in large quantities would be explained as "for sale," extra crew members would change clothes and describe themselves as passengers, and cooking boilers would be explained as distilling vats for palm oil that many legitimate traders carried.[9]

The Africa Squadron made several visits to ports in Liberia during October, November and December, 1843, with the objective of supporting the American settlements there and fostering trade. The American Colonization Society had purchased tracts of land along the African coast between Sierra Leone and Cape Palmas for receiving colonies of American Negroes. Monrovia, the capital of Liberia, by 1843 had become a neat colonial capital with stone houses, as well as American cultural and political standards. The Africa Squadron arrived at Cape Palmas on October 19, 1843. Here the Maryland branch of the American Colonization Society had established a colony in 1834 called "Maryland in Africa," with villages named Harper and Tubman after benefactors of the Society. Maryland in Africa had both Catholic and Episcopalian missions, and an American-educated governor named John Brown Russwurm. Russwurm, a graduate of Bowdoin College and a former editor of a Negro newspaper in New York, had become governor of African Maryland in 1836. His community then comprised about 650 colonists. The natives had villages of conical huts nearby. Maryland in Africa continued to struggle to survive, later becoming the County of Maryland in Liberia in 1857.[10]

The coast of West Africa was a treacherous place for merchant ships hoping to trade there. The tribes on the coast had a financial advantage over the interior tribes because they could trade with the visiting ships and then sell the foreign goods to the inland tribes for a profit. Thus, warfare occurred among the tribes over occupancy of the beach areas. The Fishmen, an interior tribe, had been able to overcome the Berebee people along about ten miles of the coast and had built five villages there. At first they preyed on canoes passing their area of the beach, and as they grew bolder they started attacking foreign ships. Two American ships had been attacked, the *Edward Burley* and the *Mary Carver*. Military action by the United States squadron was needed.

On November 27, 1843, the Squadron visited Sinu, just to the west of African Maryland, in order to see that justice was done following a fight between natives and sailors of the American schooner, *Edward Burley*. Sinu was the new home of about one hundred freedmen from Mississippi. An important meeting took place among the native chiefs, Commodore Perry, Captains Mayo, Tattnall and Abbot and the

Governor of Liberia, Joseph J. Roberts. A force of seventy-five seamen and marines landed from thirteen boats. The landing was done with great ceremony in order to impress the natives. They rowed ashore, all in line, with flags flying. Once ashore, the sailors and marines marched to the Methodist Church, the meeting place, with accompanying music. The meeting was held with the officers on one side of the table and 20 kings on the other. The facts brought out at the meeting revealed that Captain Burke of the *Edward Burley*, in retaliation for an African doing him out of $4, seized two native canoes and imprisoned their crews. He then sent his mate and cook in the schooner's boat, armed, in pursuit of a third canoe. The natives killed these two men. The killers were from the Fishman tribe, not the Sinu tribe. The group of officers concluded that Burke had been the aggressor, but that the murders were unjustified. The Commodore ordered the Fishmen's town to be burned and kept three hostages to be sent to Monrovia. Soon, one of the murderers was apprehended, and later the colonists chased the tribesmen back to the bush.[11]

The Squadron soon returned to Maryland in Africa because of the approach of a hostile tribe which threatened to destroy that colony. The naval officers were about to sit down to dinner at Governor Russwurm's house when an alarm gun sounded from the colonists' fort on Mount Tubman, and a breathless messenger announced that the Berebee tribe was attacking. The officers and thirty marines rushed to the site and found that the attack had been repulsed by the garrison. Apparently, the report of a saluting cannon that morning had suggested to the Berebee that a war was on between Maryland and her neighbor, King Freeman, so they had decided to move in to share the spoil. The naval officers soon thereafter held a meeting with King Freeman who was dressed in his crimson damask robe with gold lace, and he agreed there would be no more trouble.[12]

The next episode occurred during a later visit to Berebee just to the east of Cape Palmas. It was at Berebee, about two years earlier, that the American ship, *Mary Carver*, with a cargo worth $12,000, had anchored off a Fishmen village to trade with the natives. The Captain had gone ashore, was assaulted, and killed by the Fishmen. The natives stole all the cargo, destroyed the ship, and murdered her crew. A conference aboard the *Macedonian* of the naval officers and the governors of Maryland in Africa and Liberia determined that reparations should be required and the criminals tried by their fellow tribesmen.[13]

A subsequent visit to the royal capital of the Fishmen on Dec. 11, 1843, proved quite a hazardous undertaking. The Americans intended to ask that the royal capital be removed from the area. The landing group was met on the beach by fifty natives armed with muskets, war spears, huge wooden fish-harpoons and broad knives. The capital was palisaded with a meeting house at the center. Most of the warriors were out of sight and thought to be in ambush. No women or children were evident in the village. Marines were posted at the gates, and other groups of sailors and marines were placed at the opposite ends of the capital village. King Krako, described as "a monstrous fellow with a sinister expression," wore a beautiful robe and carried a short curved sword with a blade six inches wide. He denied all charges and, touching his ears and tongue symbolically to his sword, signaled that he was willing to attend a meeting in two days at Berebee.

On December 13, 1843, a landing was mounted by the Americans in an impressive manner. They gathered all boats of the squadron alongside the *Macedonian* off Little Berebee. The Captains of the ships and about two hundred marines and sailors boarded the boats, and rowed for the shore, line abreast. In order to avoid entering a village of hostile natives, the navy personnel pitched a tent on the beach for meetings. King Ben Krako, a large, strong black, and five or six of his men came to the meeting conducted through an interpreter. The interpreter was one of the murderers. Krako's defense was so unbelievable that Perry ordered the marines to approach. The interpreter started to run when he heard a warning shot from the nearby village. Commander Tattnall shot him before he ran far. Krako then tried to get away. Perry seized him by his long calico robe which carried away, then grabbed the royal loincloth and was dragged through the sand for several yards. At that point a sailor hit Krako with the butt end of his gun and others jabbed him with bayonets. He pretended to be dead, but seeing a musket on the ground, leaped to get it. Captain Mayo lunged at the same time, but Krako got the musket and grappled with Mayo. Mayo gave Krako a mortal stab with his pistol bayonet. The natives then opened fire on the Americans from the woods area. The hostiles were quite close, but could hit nothing with their old, rusty muskets. During this skirmish, Mayo received a severe burn on the face as a result of the discharge of a native's gun. Mayo in his record of service describes the encounter as follows: "personal encounter with King Crakoo (also known as King Rahee) [Krako]; in this engagement was severely burnt in the face by a discharge of the Berrebyan muskets."

The landing party finally drove the Fishmen out of their

village and burned it, while the guns of the Squadron lent fire support. All Americans were re-embarked with no loss. They took the dying Krako on board the *Macedonian*, but he did not live long. The next day the squadron went to Grand Berebee to meet with various kings, who disclaimed any part in the *Mary Carver* episode and agreed with the killing of the "bad" man, Krako. They then signed an agreement to refrain from plundering trading ships or molesting missionaries. In return, prisoners captured several months earlier by the brig, *Porpoise*, were returned. The Americans gave sailor suits to the kings, along with other gifts and Prince Jumbo, a king's son, received an officer's frock coat. The Treaty of Grand Berebee was never violated.[14]

Running low on supplies towards the end of December, 1843, the Squadron returned to the Cape Verde Islands, stopping off at Cape Palmas and Monrovia enroute. Thereafter, Mayo and Abbot of the *Decatur* exchanged commands, and Mayo returned to the United States in command of *Decatur*.[15] Presumably the exchange was made because of the injuries to Captain Mayo. In addition, his son, Theodoric Bland Mayo, 2 years old, had died during his absence on September 19, 1843.

Mayo thus had a rather short tour in Africa; his old ship the *Macedonian* did not return to New York until April 28, 1845. Mayo remained in command of the *Decatur* until January 9, 1845. Shortly after his departure from *Decatur* the Navy appointed him to a Board of Examination to be convened at the Philadelphia Naval Asylum to determine which midshipmen were entitled for promotion and to act as an advisory council for Secretary of the Navy Bancroft with respect to the proposed naval school.

The U. S. Naval Academy is unique among the military

academies in that there was no law passed that authorized its establishment. There were many aborted attempts to establish the school from 1814 when it was first suggested by William Jones, Secretary of the Navy, under President Madison. Repeated efforts were made by Congress to pass a law to start a naval school. Once, in 1826, it failed by a single vote in the Senate. In January, 1826, the Maryland Legislature passed a resolution requesting the Maryland congressional group to "call the attention of their respective houses to the superior advantages which the city of Annapolis and its neighborhood possesses as a situation for a Naval Academy."

George Bancroft became Secretary of the Navy in 1845, and he had a clever plan to circumvent the Congress. He realized that he could save money from the fund marked "instruction" by putting large numbers of instructors on unpaid vacation, then using the money to establish the school with a few of the best instructors. His first step to implement the plan was to get support from the senior leadership of the Navy. It was at that time that Bancroft appointed an advisory board to recommend a location for the naval school. In addition to Captain Isaac Mayo, Commodores George C. Read, Thomas Ap. C. Jones, Matthew Perry and Captain E.A.F. Lavellette were on the board.

Mayo is often given credit for locating the U.S. Naval Academy in Annapolis. The sequence of events in choosing the site are described below. In the appointment letter to the board, Secretary Bancroft said that Fort Severn had been suggested, especially as a vessel could be stationed there to serve as a school of gunnery. One author wrote that three locations were seriously considered: Annapolis, Newport, Rhode Island, and League Island in the Virginia portion of the Chesapeake Bay. Two of the five initially favored each of the Newport and Virginia locations; but apparently Mayo convinced them that Annapolis was the best choice.[16] The following from Park Benjamin's book about the U. S. Naval Academy describes a slightly different version of the decision on location: "They were entirely harmonious in agreeing upon a Southern location, but Captain Mayo lived at Annapolis, and as Professor Lockwood says, 'believed that the world revolved around that place.' Whether Mayo suggested the idea of selecting a site at the Maryland capital, or whether it was a remembrance of the old resolution of 1826 of the Legislature of that State, coupled with Secretary Bancroft's economical notion of using an obsolete army post when nothing better seemed obtainable, it is needless here to inquire. Perry always voted with Mayo on general principles. Jones saw nothing good outside of Virginia, where he came from, and he, with another, insisted on an island at the mouth of the Elizabeth River. The others preferred islands in the Chesapeake Bay. They debated the matter for twelve days, and finally Jones and Mayo managed to agree on Annapolis, whereupon the rest acceded."[17]

In the reply to Secretary of the Navy from the President of the Board, George C. Read, he wrote "Three of the undersigned are ignorant of the precise situation of Fort Severn, and its fitness for a naval school....., but they are told by their associates, Commodore Jones and Captain Mayo that the fort embraces sufficient space and the harbor and neighboring shores offer all the requisite advantages for gun practice and evolution of steamers and boats."[18] Shortly thereafter, Bancroft appointed another board of three officers representing the younger element of the Navy to review the plans for a naval school, to give its recommendation on a site and to recommend the personnel at the school. The second board endorsed the Annapolis location.

Fort Severn was transferred to the Navy on August, 15, 1845, and on October 10th the school was opened. Recognition by Congress that the school existed came when they received the annual report from the Secretary of the Navy. In the report Bancroft reported that a naval school was in full operation in Annapolis. An appropriation of $28, 200 was voted for continuance of the institution. Thus, the Naval Academy backed into existence.[19]

There are differing accounts on how the decision was reached to select Annapolis as the site of the Naval School, but in both accounts it is clear that Isaac Mayo played a pivotal role and should be recognized for his important contribution to the U.S. Naval Academy.

.

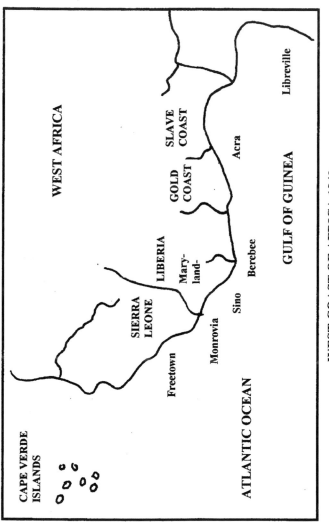

CAPE VERDE
ISLANDS

WEST AFRICA

SIERRA
LEONE

LIBERIA

Mary-
land-

GOLD
COAST

SLAVE
COAST

Acra

Libreville

Freetown

Monrovia

Sino

Berebee

ATLANTIC OCEAN

GULF OF GUINEA

WEST COAST OF AFRICA 1843

Navy Museum

USS MACEDONIAN-COMMANDED BY MAYO IN AFRICA, 1843

Courtesy of Old South River Club

CAPTAIN ISAAC MAYO - ABOUT 1845

9
Mexican War
1847

*"Your friend Mayo is one of
the bravest men I ever knew."*
General Scott to James Fenimore Cooper, 1850

By the time of the Mexican War Isaac Mayo had already served in the Navy for thirty-eight years and was one of the Navy's more senior captains. The war with Mexico was the first major conflict during most of the naval officers' careers, and no one wanted to miss the opportunity to fight.

Captain Mayo was assigned to command the *USS Mississippi* on March 3, 1847. *Mississippi* would serve as the flagship of the Gulf Squadron under the command of Commodore Matthew C. Perry. Perry, who had been the Commanding Officer of the *Mississippi* from September, 1846, was designated the Vice-Commodore of the Gulf Squadron. The *Mississippi* had returned to Norfolk from the Gulf of Mexico in mid-January, 1847, to have her boilers overhauled.[1] The Navy ordered Commodore Perry to relieve Commodore Conners on Perry's return to the Gulf. Thus, at the request of Perry, he and Mayo were joined together once again. Captain Mayo had served as the commanding officer of the flagship in the African Squadron under Perry, and they had both again served together on the board to select a site for the U. S. Naval Academy.

The *Mississippi*, newly constructed in Philadelphia, was two-hundred and twenty-nine feet long, with a draft of 19 feet, and a displacement of 1692 tons. She carried two 10-inch and eight 8-inch shell guns of the Paixhans type. [Paixhans were shell throwing guns invented by the Stevens of Hoboken in 1814 and further developed by a French artillery officer named Paixhans. The Paixhans were far more destructive than the old round shot guns, but did not have the range, so that both were used on ships for some time.] The *Mississippi* was barque-rigged with 19,000 square feet of sail. She had a coal-burning power plant, operating two side-lever engines, connected to two paddlewheels, each 28 feet in diameter. A serious weakness in the machinery plant design required the use of salt water in the boilers because there was no fresh-water-making capability on the ship. The boilers were supposed to be cleaned every eight months. Cleaning couldn't be done on that schedule because of operating demands, so the boilers leaked seriously most of the time. Nevertheless, in twenty years service in two wars and two voyages around the world, *Mississippi* never got into serious trouble until she ran aground off Port Hudson, blew up and sank in 1863.[2]

For Captain Mayo command of the *Mississippi* was a prize assignment, especially during war. The war between the United States and Mexico formally began in May, 1846. It was prompted by the annexation of Texas by the United States and our ambition to annex California. The war was not popular in the East, but was popular in the West and lower South. The Whig party, including Henry Clay, Daniel Webster and John C. Calhoun, opposed President Polk, a Democrat, who favored the war.

The United States Navy, as usual, was poorly prepared. They had several fine new frigates, sloops and brigs built to fight a blue-water war, but lacked light-draft steamers and sailing vessels for operation along the Gulf Coast and in the rivers of Mexico.

The naval war in Mexico proceeded at a slow pace during the years before Commodore Perry was placed in charge and Mayo arrived with him in *Mississippi*. Their orders directed them to blockade the Mexican coast. The climate conditions in the area were miserable. In the summer during the rainy season, fever-bearing mosquitoes were prevalent, transmitting malaria and yellow fever. Gales from the north accompanied by heavy rain frequently presented problems in the winter. A series of raids on river cities (Tabasco, Tampico, Carmen) by the U. S. Navy in 1846 resulted in the capture of a number of small vessels that could be used by the Navy.[3] On March 9, 1847, a landing was made by U. S. forces at Veracruz. It was a major amphibious landing by the U. S. Army, supported by the U. S. Navy and Marines. General Scott, in command of the Army at Veracruz, was a man of great ego, and was greatly frustrated by his lack of ordnance to batter down the walls of Veracruz. His plan was to demonstrate that success and glory could be attained with a minimum loss of life, the reverse of General Taylor, the commander of the left wing assault on Mexico. Commodore Perry and Captain Mayo arrived off Veracruz eleven days later, on March 20, 1847, in *Mississippi*, and Commodore Perry took command of the Gulf Squadron.

The first day, March 21, 1847, proved an eventful one for Mayo. He received word that *S.S. Hunter*, together with

Jeine Nelly, a captured French blockade runner, and a pilot schooner, had grounded in the breakers on the northeast side of Isla
Verde, a few miles offshore from Sacrificios. The shipwrecked
vessels had sixty people on board, including a mother and child.
With a severe gale, sailing ships could not leave their moorings;
even *Mississippi* had parted her cables in the severe wind and
seas. Regardless, Mayo raised steam and got underway into the
gale. A British war steamer much nearer the scene of disaster did
not respond. Upon arrival, Captain Mayo, four officers and several seamen volunteered to man the *Mississippi* barge to make
the rescue. They successfully rescued all the people after several
trips through rough seas.[4]

Before the arrival of Perry and Mayo in *Mississippi*,
General Scott, on March 18, 1847, had opened fire on Veracruz
with the few small caliber guns available to the Army. Commodore Perry offered to land heavy shell guns from the Navy
ships, provided they could be manned by Navy officers and
men. General Scott turned him down, insisting on the use of
Army personnel. After several days of frustration, Scott agreed
to the terms, and the Navy prepared to land their guns. Seven
U.S. gunboats, *Falcon, Reefer, Vixen, Petrel, Boneta, Spitfire*, and *Tampico*, opened an assault on March 22, 1847. The
bombardment continued the next day. Mexican gunners fired
back at the ships with many near misses. When Commodore
Perry sent the order to retire, Captain Tattnall chose not to
see it and continued the attack. Perry then sent Captain Mayo
in a small boat through enemy gunfire to give a positive order
to retire. No casualties resulted to the small gunboats or to
Mayo's crew.[5]

On the night of the 23rd, the Navy landed six heavy
guns from the ship batteries and a detachment who pulled the

guns by hand over the sand hills. Detachments from each ship, each led by a Lieutenant, and the entire Navy group commanded by a Captain, manned and fired the guns. Captain Aulick commanded the naval batteries ashore until 2 p.m..on the 24th, when he was relieved by Captain Mayo with a fresh detachment of sailors and additional ammunition. On the 25th the Army and Navy guns continued the bombardment until about 2:30 p.m., when the Mexican guns stopped firing. Mayo noted in his report to Commodore Perry that two Mexican batteries on their extreme left then fired on them, but after a brisk return fire they stopped at about 3:30 p.m.

The naval battery, consisting of three 68-pound 8-inch shell (Paixhans) guns, during this day had breached the wall and had destroyed many houses in the rear. Naval guns had fired a total of 1000 shells and 800 round shot, almost half of all fired from U. S. cannon. Mayo observed the Mexicans evacuating the fort. He had hoped for a better battle and ordered his men to stand on the parapet and give three cheers, saying, "If the enemy intends to fire another shot, our cheers will draw it...." He then mounted a horse and galloped off to report to Commodore Perry on the beach. En route he encountered General Scott at Army headquarters and predicted that the enemy would never fire another shot. Mayo was so warmly embraced by the General that he was nearly pulled off the horse. Scott thanked him in the name of the Army for the day's work and praised him profusely, commenting that the post of honor and of danger had been assigned by Scott to the Navy. General Scott then said, "I had my eye upon you, Captain Mayo, as Midshipman, as a Lieutenant, as a Captain, now let me thank you personally as Commodore Mayo for this day's work." Of course, the Navy did not confirm this spot promotion. [It is probable that Scott was referring to the *Hornet-Peacock* and *Hornet-Penguin* battles in the War of 1812.] Mayo then galloped on to report to Perry. Veracruz did surrender, and the formal ceremony took place on March 29th.[6]

It is probably the series of episodes at Veracruz (rescue of the *Hunter's* shipwrecked crew through heavy seas, notification to withdraw delivered by Mayo to Tattnall under heavy shore battery fire, and successful bombardment of the Veracruz walls) that led General Scott to compliment Mayo years later. James Fenimore Cooper wrote to Isaac Mayo in February, 1850, in New York City that General Scott had told him Mayo was, "one of the bravest men he ever knew. "[7]

Isaac Mayo participated in two additional actions in Mexico before he was detached from command of *Mississippi* at his request to attend to personal business at home. In the first action no actual warfare was involved. General Scott wanted to take Alvarado, the principal market town for horse and beef cattle south of Veracruz. He sent the Army under General Quitman, and the Navy sent a single steamer armed with a single gun. When the steamer arrived ahead of the Army and fired its gun a few times, the town surrendered. A midshipman and two enlisted men held the town until the Army arrived. The General was greatly amused by the incident. Sixty guns were found at Alvarado; thirty-five were shipped as trophies and twenty-five were destroyed.

Captain Mayo's part in this was to be appointed Governor of Alvarado. His duty included rounding up horses for the Army and maintaining the peace. In his report Captain Mayo says that he subdued the towns Talascoya and Cosamopaya when several cantons sent in their submission in order to avoid having armed force sent after them. He also said,

"On the 12th of May I fitted out an expedition against Holescogan consisting of about 80 officers, seamen and marines from this flotilla under my command at this place, having a twelve pound carronade mounted upon two canoes lashed together." The next day the town was taken. He stayed in Alvarado for only a short time, probably from the end of March to the end of May, 1847.[8]

Mayo's final duty in Mexico was as Adjutant General to Commodore Perry in an amphibious attack on Tabasco (now called Villahermosa). Commodore Perry organized the first infantry brigade in the history of the Navy. He had over 2000 volunteers from the men aboard ship who had been drilled by their own officers aboard ship or on the beach. It was part of this group who started up the Tabasco River (now called Grijalva) toward Tabasco (Villahermosa) on June 14, 1847. The first effort was to cross the sand bar at the entrance to the river. The *Mississippi* and sailing frigates anchored outside the sand bar; steamers *Scourge*, *Scorpion*, *Spitfire*, and *Vixen* then towed across two bomb brigs and two schooners. They returned to tow across ships' boats and surfboats crammed with men. There were a total of 1084 seamen and marines in forty boats. Commodore Perry and Captain Mayo aboard the temporary flagship, *Scorpion*, proceeded upstream all night and the following day.

As the flagship reached the elbow of Devil's Bend on June 15th, the guns of at least a hundred enemy fired a volley. The awnings of the *Scorpion* where Perry and Mayo were standing were dented and splintered, but no one was injured. The order was given to fire; cavalry could be seen beyond the shoreline when a ten-inch shell from *Vesuvius* exploded among them scattering all the Mexicans. Perry's group anchored for the night.

On the morning of the 16th, Perry decided to land on the river bank rather than attempt to remove underwater obstacles placed in the river by the Mexicans . They selected a bluff next to a spot called Seven Palms. While accompanying ships shot grape, musket shot, and shells, the landing force of 80 officers and 1015 men were led ashore by Commodore Perry accompanied by Captain Mayo. Both men drew their swords and led the charge up the bluff. When they reached the top, they unfurled the Commodore's flag in sight of the loaded boats. All the men cheered and followed the officers' lead to land on the shore. The landing force worked its way up the river bank The guns had to be hauled by hand across swamp in some places, and the heat was excessive. One officer later wrote that it was heartbreaking and backbreaking work and many men succumbed. Commander Buchanan reported in a letter, "Many of the officers carried canteens with liquor and the moment they saw a poor fellow fall they would give him a drop of comfort which had an astonishing effect on him." Meanwhile, the ships cleared the underwater obstacles and moved upstream.

The first shore battle occurred at Acachapan breastwork held by 300 Mexican infantry, 300 cavalry and two guns. The Americans fired a few rounds of shot and then charged. The Mexicans abandoned their positions and fled toward Tabasco (Villahermosa). Meanwhile, the American ship forces reached Fort Iturbide and suffered several hits from the fire from the fort. The ships passed the fort and fired backwards into it with good results. An officer from one of the ships landed with 68 men and forced abandonment of the fort by the Mexicans. When the ships reached Tabasco (Villahermosa), they found it undefended. The landing force arrived at the town at about 3:30 p.m. that day after it had been surrendered to the ships.

The amphibious force had taken the last Mexican town on the Gulf at the cost of only five men wounded. Out of a Mexican force of at least 1400 men, some thirty were killed. The American force remained at Tabasco (Villahermosa) five days, destroying munitions and fortifications, and then returned to their ships outside the sand bar.[9] Captured cannons were taken aboard the vessels. Three of the cannons were sent to the Naval School in Annapolis by Buchanan, its first superintendent. Buchanan also brought home four large shells as souvenirs and placed them at the gate posts his home in Easton, Maryland, which he called "The Rest."[10] This battle may be a source of the cannons and cannon balls placed at Gresham by Captain Mayo discussed later. Tabasco was abandoned by the Americans on July 22nd because of the widespread yellow fever and continuing trouble with Mexican guerrillas. This was the last important naval engagement of the Mexican War. In fact, the Navy had finished its work after capturing every port on the eastern coast of Mexico and establishing a strict blockade on the country.

Captain Mayo was detached from the *Mississippi* on July 10, 1847, to return home aboard the *USS Albany*. He had served in the Mexican War for only about 4 months, yet he had participated in all its major naval engagements. Mayo arrived back home on August 10th. The record indicates that he was called home on personal business. His father-in-law, Theodoric Bland, had died on Nov. 16, 1846, and his will named Captain Isaac Mayo as his executor.[11] There was a considerable amount of property and money involved, including real estate in Virginia and Maryland.

Senior officers customarily brought back some things to

commemorate their service in foreign lands in those days. For example, Perry after his tour on the African Station in 1845, brought back breadfruit, and "a curious fish" from Cape Verdes, a native iron from East Africa and a mask worn by the Grand Devil from near Cape Palmas.[12] A newspaper article in the Mayo Scrapbook reports, "Among a collection of Mexican curiosities, trophies, etc. which Captain Mayo brought with him, we perceived a small, but apparently full grown deer of the Mexican breed. It is very like a gazelle and is the picture of innocence, and would answer better than the lamb for an emblem of peace. Strange that in a land of such ferocious barbarians as Mexico, such a mild, gentle creature should be born."[13]

Information from a school report done by children of Mayo Elementary School in 1952 indicates that there were two cannons and a few cannon balls at Gresham brought from Mexico by Mayo.[14] One cannon is still at Gresham. It is cast iron and stamped with "Alvarado," the place where Mayo served as Governor for a short time. The cannon is about 50 inches long, with a seven-inch bore. The outside of the barrel tapers from 14-1/2 inches diameter at the breech to 10-1/2 inches at the mouth. The opening in the breech for powder is about three inches in diameter, and the opening at the top of the breech for insertion of the ignition device is about 1/2 inch in diameter. The cannon ball that was at the gate of Gresham in 1952 is no longer there; however, it is in the possession of a private party in Mayo. The iron ball is about 13 inches in diameter, marked "San Juan de Ullo." The marking probably indicates that the ball came from San Juan de Ulloa (now Ulua), which was a castle and fort in Veracruz. The second cannon is no longer at Gresham; but is rumored to be in the area. The marking on that cannon is unknown.

The Mexican War was a strange experience for the

Navy. Their role was a support role for the Army. The young men on the Navy ships were eager for combat, and the officers had to exercise good judgment and restraint to avoid looting and attacks on civilians. Some of the older naval officers measured success by the number of killed and injured among their own crews and the enemy; fortunately, Perry and Mayo were sufficiently enlightened to know that they faced a weak enemy. The objective of establishing control of the Mexican port towns was achieved with relatively few casualties to men on either side and with little damage to U.S. ships. Victory was accomplished in a short time frame, once Perry and Mayo arrived on the scene. Probably, the most challenging part of the war was not the combat, but the climate, yellow fever, and geographical conditions. These were the kind of conditions that Mayo had come to expect after his duty in the West Indies, Brazil and Africa.

Captain Mayo received recognition for his services in the Mexican War when the Maryland legislature passed a resolution of praise "for the gallant and meritorious conduct of Marylanders who distinguished themselves in the war," however, no personal recognition of his service was awarded by the Legislature or Congress.

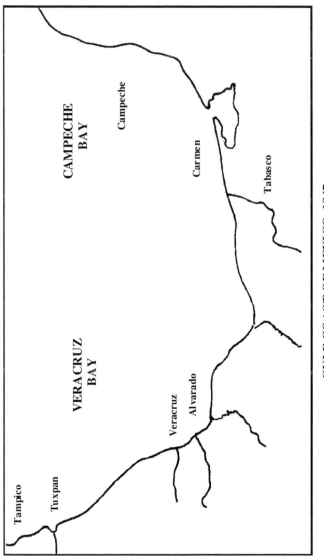

GULF COAST OF MEXICO, 1847

Lieutenant Walke

Naval Academy Museum

USS MISSISSIPPI RESCUING CREW OF HUNTER OFF VERA CRUZ ON MARCH 21, 1847. MAYO IN SMALL BOAT

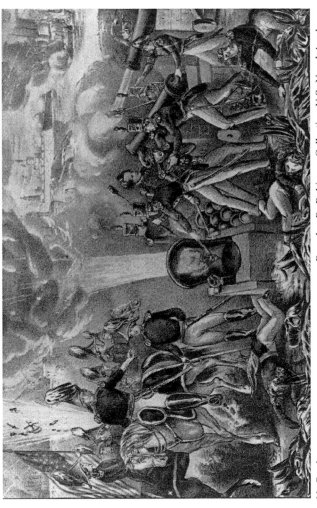

N. Currier

Beverley R. Robinson Collection U.S. Naval Academy

SIEGE OF VERA CRUZ MARCH 1847
MAYO IN COMMAND OF NAVY GUNS AND CREW

Lieutenant Walke

Naval Academy Museum

**LANDING AT TABASCO, MEXICO, JUNE 1847
MAYO AS ADJUTANT GENERAL**

10
Commodore
in *USS Constitution*
1852-1855

"Nothing could be more gratifying to my professional pride than to serve with the Constitution for my flag ship. Possessing every admirable quality that can commend a vessel to her officers and crew. Swift, strong and very commodious, her past history has endeared her to every American heart."
Letter from Isaac Mayo to the Secretary of the Navy, 1854

    The Navy assigned Captain Isaac Mayo to the *USS Constitution* as the Commodore of the African Squadron on Sept 6, 1852. He was sixty years old at the time of his assignment. This was his first duty as Commodore after 43 years in the U. S. Navy. The *USS Constitution* and Commodore Mayo did not return to the United States until June 2, 1855. The *Constitution*, the most famous of the old United States sailing ships, is preserved in Boston Harbor. The ship was launched in Boston in 1797, with a length of 175 feet at the gundeck, beam of 43.5 feet, depth of hold of 14.6 feet and draft of 23 feet aft. She carried 450 officers and men with a displacement of 2400 tons. Her nominal battery was 44 guns, but she carried 56. During the War of 1812 she defeated the *HMS Java, Guerriere, Cyane* and *Levant*. The *Constitution* was never defeated. During the Civil War she was towed from Annapolis to Newport, Rhode Island, to prevent her capture. The *Constitution* was sailed back to Annapolis after the war was over. In 1878 she took goods to Le Havre for the Paris exhibition; her last commission ended in 1884. *Constitution* was made a receiving ship in Portsmouth, New Hampshire, and in 1897 was towed to Boston to be preserved indefinitely.[1] Even though *Constitution* was already 50 years old when Mayo took command, it was a tremendous honor to be assigned as her Commodore.

Commodore Mayo first boarded and raised his broad pennant on the *Constitution* in New York City on Dec. 23, 1852. He attempted to obtain sufficient crew, without complete success, between that time and the departure of the ship from the wharf for Ellis Island on Feb. 24, 1853.[2] He carried 50 seamen on the ship for use of the other ships in the Africa Squadron and received about half the crew he needed for *Constitution*. He was authorized to touch at certain ports in the Mediterranean and was directed to transport Col. Nicholson, the Consul for Tunis, to his assignment. He sailed from New York on March 2nd after receiving powder and other armament at the magazine on Ellis Island. Upon his departure he wrote to the Secretary of the Navy, "I have not as good a crew as I could have wished for this noble ship."[3] He arrived in Gibraltar on March 23rd after a rough passage, then proceeded to Spezia (Italy), an American depot, where he delivered dispatches sent by the Navy Department. Commodore Mayo remained in port at Spezia from April 2nd to April 23rd because of bad weather. He then proceeded to Leghorn (Italy) to pick up bread (the Mediterranean squadron baked their bread there) and then to Tunis. In Tunis he received honors (gun salutes) and entertained foreign consuls, but found that Colonel Nicholson had been replaced by Dr. Heap.[4] Then he had to find a way home for Colonel Nicholson.

The ship proceeded to French Algiers. Commodore Mayo explained to the Secretary of the Navy that he hoped to find more seamen there, and it was a good place for Colonel Nicholson to find a ship headed back to the United States. Mayo observed that Algiers had improved tremendously as a seaport, including this assessment in a rather complete report about Algiers, since American ships seldom visited there. He felt Algiers had no equal in the Mediterranean, emphasizing its large harbor, plentiful facilities, friendliness of the French officials, inexpensive merchandise, and good communications with France (a packet arrived every five days). Mayo recommended the American fleet winter in that harbor. While in Algiers the announcement of the death of the Vice President of the United States, William R. King, was received, and the ship rendered military honors to his memory.

Thereafter, Mayo's departure for his station on the African Coast was delayed by adverse weather, a west wind and sea current. From Algiers he sailed to Gibraltar, then on to Tangiers to deliver messages from the American Consul in Gibraltar. In Tangiers he encountered 2000 pilgrims on their way to Mecca. Among them was the nephew of the Emperor of Morocco. Mayo showed him the *Constitution*, and he reported that he was "most impressed by the fine appearance and warlike display."[5] The *USS Constitution* finally arrived at Madeira on June 21, 1853, where she relieved the *USS John Adams*. By then Mayo had spent about 3-1/2 months in the Mediterranean area.

In his early letters to the Secretary of the Navy, Mayo attempts to establish limits on the time that ships are left on the African Station because of the poor health conditions. He wrote that the *USS Bainbridge* had been away from the United States for 2-1/2 years, far too long in his opinion. He notes, "I beg leave to call to your attention the urgent necessity of not permitting the vessels of this Squadron to remain more than two years absent from the United States. My own past experience on the Station and the concurrent testimony of all officers who have served here, point out the danger of protracted cruises on the Coast of Africa. Not that the loss of life is likely to be great, but because the constitutions of officers and men become debilitated to such a degree, as materially to impair their further usefulness in the Public Service. I hope to keep the *Constitution* very actively employed and as she has a large crew in somewhat narrow quarters, I trust that the Department will see the necessity of sending a ship to take her place in eighteen months from this time."[6] About a week later, Mayo took matters into his own hands and ordered *USS Bainbridge* to return home. He explained that her relief was expected soon, and that most of the officers and crew and been absent from the United States for three years.

On July 18, 1853, Commodore Mayo proposed to the Secretary of the Navy that he join Commodore Perry in his trip to open up Japan. He suggested that he would remain the African Squadron Commodore during the trip and would return after about four months. He wrote, "Commodore Perry and myself have seen much hard service together during the last thirty years, and it would be most agreeable to me, as I am very confident it would be to him, if we could again be associated on duty. The *Constitution* is a strong ship, well manned and equipped, and her very name alone would be a powerful reinforcement to any squadron of our Navy. I propose therefore that, orders be sent to me to sail in her during the approaching winter, in time to reach Japan before the summer weather permits the commencement of active operations on that coast, and that during those operations, I serve as second in command bearing a red pendant and holding the same relation towards Commodore Perry that he held towards Commodore Conners during a part of the Mexican War."[7]

The Navy Department reply was not received until January 8, 1854, and it is very diplomatic. That response read, "In reply to your letter you are informed that the Department is gratified with the laudable spirit evinced by you in the desire to cooperate with Commodore Perry in Japan, and regrets that it cannot accept of your service, as tendered. The Department is without information from Commodore Perry touching the necessity of additional force in the East India and China seas, added to which it would be embarrassing to diminish the force on the Coast of Africa, by taking away more than one-half the force required by Treaty Stipulations. Should anything occur, however, rendering it necessary to add to Commodore Perry's command, your application to join him shall receive careful consideration."[8]

Commodore Mayo had one more recommendation at about this same time; he recommended that a small steamer be sent to his squadron. This was one more recommendation that was not accepted. Many years later steamers were sent, and they were far more successful than sailing ships in interrupting the slave trade.[9]

It is interesting to compare the approach and actions Commodore Mayo took by his own initiative with today, when instant communications assure that any independent action by a military commander will be suitably corrected and, if appropriate, punished. Mayo's decision to send the *USS Bainbridge* home before orders were received because it was the right thing to do is impressive. He reported that he had taken in tow a British schooner, *George*, had towed it two hundred miles from Sierra Leone to St. Vincent, and had supplied her with water and provisions because she was in great distress. He could have done nothing and avoided the risk of criticism from the Navy Department. He also, on his own authority, appointed an American consul in the port of St. Paul de Loandz, Angola (owned by Portugal), on a temporary basis with the idea that he would be able to identify American vessels in the slave trade by examining their papers. He later appointed a temporary consul to the British colony Bathurst near the Gambia River. Of course, these appointments were State Department business, but he saw the necessity and took action. In late February, 1854, he sent the *USS Perry* to Norfolk, rather than have her return to Port Praya. He explained that she had been there for two years and it was just as fast to go to Norfolk as it was to return to Port Praya because of the prevailing wind. Such initiatives would be impossible in today's Navy.[10]

Commodore Mayo considered it part of his job to protect U.S. commercial interests and to aid the U. S.-sponsored colonies along the African Coast to which he was assigned. He wrote a summary of the situation in Africa to the Secretary of the Navy on August 22, 1853, as follows: "When I left this station in the latter part of 1844, an important trade with the United States had grown up under the protecting influence of our Squadron. The energy and shrewdness of our countrymen enabled them to contend successfully with their English competition and this trade continued to increase until within the last year, when the British Government, with its usual policy, brought the great motive power of the age, to develop the hidden resources of this rich continent and drive all commercial rivals from the field that promises such an ample harvest.

"Steamers, receiving a considerable sum for the transportation of the mails, leave England on the 24th of every
month and touching at the many ports on the coast, between
the Gambia and Fernandoto, have given a wonderful impetus
to their languishing trade. These steamers have succeeded
beyond all expectations, and bid fair to prove to their owners
a most profitable investment. The traders on the coast who
had depended for their supplies, chiefly from transient vessels
from the U.S., now order them from England; calculating almost to an hour, the time when they will be received. The
returning steamer enables them to send back at a fixed period
the produce of the country that has accumulated in their hands.

"As a citizen of the South and a large land and
slaveholder, I have long watched with interest the progress of
the 'Colonization' and my personal observation of its success
in Liberia has made me one of its staunchest advocates. A line
of steamers between Africa and one of our Southern ports
will furnish invaluable aid to this great cause and will gain for
our country that most valuable trade which, while yet in its
infancy, was fast falling into our hands when the foresight of
the British Government and the efforts of the British merchants snatched it from us. In conclusion, it may not be amiss
for me to draw the attention of the Department to the fact that
as the lawful trade increases upon the Coast, the petty Kings
and Chiefs can procure by honest means of purchasing what they
desire, and thus are deprived of their chief inducement to furnish
victims for the slave trade, upon which they have hitherto relied."[11]

Thus, Commodore Mayo was suggesting a far-sighted
solution to the slave-trade problem. It is doubtful that these
steps, by themselves, would have prevented outlaw chiefs from
seeking easy money, but had it been possible to build prosperous

colonies along the African Coast, they may have been able to police and reduce slave trade themselves.

In September, 1853, Commodore Mayo interceded in a war between two tribes that had been warring for three years and disrupting the American colonies, as well as local shipping. The two tribes, the Grebo and the Barbo, lived on opposite sides of the Cavally River. The *Constitution* sailed to the Cavally River, where Commodore Mayo sent a messenger to contact the two tribes. The Grebo were cooperative, but the Barbo threatened to kill the messenger. The Commodore then took five armed boats to the area and sent in a messenger with a white flag. Again the Barbo "rudely repelled my messenger and defied my power, daring me to land, and using terms which, among themselves, are considered equivalent to a declaration of war." Mayo then threw a few light signal rockets over their town to drive the women and children to the forest and from the landing gun fired a few shells over houses. The natives hung a white flag and expressed their willingness for peace. The next day delegations from the two tribes boarded *Constitution*, where they agreed on peace. Mayo reported that he had reason to believe that his intervention would save many lives, make the coast safer for merchant vessels and would bring the blessing of peace to two large tribes, whose whole attention for the last three years had been devoted to war.[12]

In November, 1853, Commodore Mayo wrote a long letter about the Africa Squadron and the American slavers operating in the area. He had just captured the American Schooner *Gambrill* and sent her home as a prize because of the clear evidence that she was employed in the slave trade. He wrote, "the slave trade is reviving on this Southern Coast and the American flag extensively used in the prosecution. Several cargoes of slaves have recently been carried off in American vessels, which having regular papers, defy the English cruisers and hope to elude the vigilance of our Squadron, knowing that it consists of only three vessels serving on a coast of great extent and dependent for its provisions upon our depot at Porto Praya, in going to and from which, much time is unavoidably consumed. Information concerning the movements of all vessels of war is carried along the coast by slave dealers with wonderful celerity and the Masters of the slave vessels are provided with every expedient to avoid capture by means of double sets of papers and flags and every other device that experience and interest can suggest."[13]

Isaac Mayo's journal for his time on *Constitution* contains a seven-page statement of evidence supporting the taking of the *Gambrill*. It was important to be completely sure that the ship taken was a slaver, because Mayo could be personally sued, if he were wrong. Portions of the statement are excerpted: "On boarding the American Schooner *H.N. Gambrill* this morning I found her papers apparently formal and correct, but could not find a cargo list.........In the caboose house I found a very large copper boiler recently set in brick work-such a copper as would be required to cook the food for slaves. On opening the hatches, I found a deck of loose hemlock boards, laid smoothly and carefully upon the tiers of casks, which upon examination were found to contain provisions and several thousand gallons of water.

"The cook, at last, told me the whole story of the voyage as he knew it. He had shipped to go in the Schooner on an honest trading voyage to the coast of Africa, but after going on board he was somewhat surprised to find that she was

detained six days, and that the crew were not allowed to commu-
nicate with the shore. At length the captain made his appearance
accompanied by a Spanish passenger, and they went to sea. On
the passage the cargo excited his suspicions, and he asked the
steward what he thought of the strange quantity of water on board,
etc. At last the steward talked with the captain about it, and the
captain admitted that he was going for slaves.

"They sailed from the Congo Nov. 1st and yesterday;
they knocked down the bulkhead which separated the fore-
castle from the hold, broke up a part of the men's chests, threw
overboard their old clothes, empty barrels, etc., in order to
make room, and laid the slave deck, ready for the reception of
the Negroes. They moved their quarters from forward to aft,
they then got up a big box, took from it the copper for cooking, and set it in brick work in the caboose house. All doubt
was then removed as to the object of the voyage.

"When the *Constitution* was discovered from the mast-
head this morning, the Captain examined her with his glass
and declared she was a Brig he had seen in the Congo. When
he found out it was a Frigate, it was too late to run away. This
is the story of the cook."[14]

An interesting controversy concerns the crew and
Captain of the *Gambrill*. Commodore Mayo deliberately allowed all but two of the crew to escape ashore. Only two
were returned to New York with the *Gambrill*. The District
Attorney of New York complained to the Navy Department
that the crew should have been returned and prosecuted; the
Navy Department did not comment, but sent the letter to
Commodore Mayo. His explanation of his actions in this regard is quite revealing: He points out that only the Captain
was an American citizen, and that the crew were people "of
abandoned lives and desperate character" that would have

required a large prize crew to avoid recapture of the vessel. He was able to return the *Gambrill* with a prize crew of mostly invalids. Mayo also indicated that "although the guilt of the *Gambrill* was evident to him; great doubts as to her condemnation were expressed by persons whose opinions I could not lightly disregard and I freely admit that I was unwilling to send these miscreants home to give the harpies that infest the functions of our Courts an opportunity to bring vexatious suits during my absence, and seize upon my property which is tangible and open to their reclamations." He also reminded the Department that the British followed this practice of releasing the slave crews. Finally, he stated that "he had judiciously used the discretionary power always given to a Commander, and particularly necessary upon this station, and that he "had acted in the best interest of the Country." The Navy Department informed him that it was gratified by the activity displayed in suppressing the slave trade as manifested in the capture of the *Gambrill*.[15]

Commodore Mayo, once more, recommended that the *Constitution* be sent home and replaced with several smaller vessels and a steamer sent to him as a flagship. This theme recurred in many of his letters, as these ships could be better deployed along the coast to catch the slavers. He adds, "Nothing could be more gratifying to my professional pride than to serve with the Constitution for my flag ship. Possessing every admirable quality that can commend a vessel to her officers and crew. Swift, strong and very commodious, her past history has endeared her to every American heart, especially to the heart of every American seaman. Were I to listen to the promptings of my own interest, I would do false to those of my government, and I therefore feel compelled to state that she is entirely unfit for the duty on which she is at present employed." He further discusses the disadvantages, saying that purchasing supplies for such a large ship is a problem, her lofty sails placed her in sight of the small slave vessels, and that her deep draft prevented her from pursuing slave ships in shallow water.[16] In a later letter he points out that the British employed twenty-six vessels, later reduced to nine, to do the job he was being asked to do with three ships. Despite these problems his reports were filled with inspections of American ships suspected of being involved in the slave trade. Mayo was receiving intelligence from the British ships and people ashore. Several ships were named as suspicious with the request that they be inspected in the U.S. Mayo asked to be relieved as Commodore in September, 1854, which would mark the two-year anniversary of his assignment as Commodore of the Africa Squadron In the same letter he wrote of the death of his wife's close relative and a large land inheritance required his presence. These events probably refer to his wife's disabled brother, William Glenn Bland.[17]

Toward the end of his cruise to Africa, Commodore Mayo received word from another officer on the *USS Constitution* that Mayo would soon be placed on the retired list. This word came to that officer in a letter from a "nine hundred dollar clerk," who worked in the Bureau of Yards and Docks, and who was originally from Baltimore. Mayo was humiliated and felt that the rumor undermined his authority as Squadron Commander. He was insulted that a man with his experience and record would be considered for retirement. He wrote both an official letter to the Secretary of the Navy and a personal letter to the Commodore of the Bureau of Yards and Docks concerning this anecdotal report.[18] These letters provide much of what is known about the personal life of Isaac Mayo and excerpts are included in Chapter One.

Commodore Mayo received orders to leave the African station with his ship, the *Constitution*, on April 1, 1855.

The ultimate demonstration of his dedication and initiative occurred during the return trip. When he was about four days out from Portsmouth, New Hampshire, where he had been directed to report, he met an American ship whose Commander and newspapers aboard led Commodore Mayo to believe that there was an impending war in Cuba, and that all available men-of-war were being sent there. Mayo diverted his ship to Cuba, arriving there on May 16, 1855. Nothing of import was happening there, so he then went to Key West to meet with Commodore McCauley. He arrived there on May 23, 1855, and found that he was not needed there either. Commodore McCauley wrote to him, "the zeal you have evinced is highly deserving of commendation, and that from the course you have pursued it is apparent that our Government has cause to place much confidence in your judgment and true patriotism."[19] Apparently this diversion to Cuba caused considerable trouble on *Constitution*. Mayo reported later that fifty-one seamen reported sick on the day after his diversion to Cuba without any sign of sickness. He punished them with one day confinement and then made sure they were not discharged with the rest of the crew, but instead were made to remain in the Navy for the rest of their period of enlistment.[20]

Commodore Mayo, judged by his words and deeds during his Naval career, can be characterized as proud of his heritage and his accomplishments, wise in the ways of the Navy bureaucracy, anxious to do his duty, and willing to take professional and personal risks as a true patriot.

11

Assessment of
Isaac Mayo's Career

"One precedent creates another, they soon
accumulate, what yesterday was fact, today
is doctrine, examples are supposed to justify
the most dangerous measures, and where they
do not suit exactly, the defect is supplied by analogy."
Junious. Isaac Mayo's Journal

Isaac Mayo's life in the U.S. Navy can be compared to that of a contemporary, Commodore Matthew Calbraith Perry. The comparison should provide some perspective on their nearly fifty years of association, while both strived for a heroic legacy. Matthew Perry became well-known; Isaac Mayo remained relatively obscure. Now, after over one hundred and forty years, the separate, yet combined effects of their different roads taken, and perhaps the role of sheer chance become more clear.

Isaac Mayo entered the U.S. Navy in 1809, was first assigned to a ship in 1810, left his last ship assignment in 1855, and was dismissed from the Naval service in 1861. During this phase of our country's history, military officers were subject to extended periods of leave between assignments, so not all of his 52 years were active Navy duty. His active duty time between 1809 and 1861 amounted to 25 years and 39 days (all but 4 months was sea duty) according to his official record in the National Archives.[1] Sixteen of those years were as a junior officer. The remainder of the time, during sporadic intervals, Isaac Mayo was on leave at his home, Gresham, located between the Rhode and South Rivers in southern Anne Arundel County.

Matthew Perry entered the Navy as a Midshipman about one year before Mayo and remained active until his death in 1858, three years prior to Mayo's dismissal and death. However, Perry had only one three-year period of inactive service during which time he served on his father-in-law's merchant ships. He was assigned to U.S. Naval stations during all of his other time ashore. For example, he had two tours in New York City, the first for nine years and the second for three and one-half years. In addition, there was a two-year tour in Boston. His official record indicates that he had 25 years of sea duty and 18 years, 11 months of shore duty. The reasons for this disparity between the two men's Navy assignments are unclear. One possibility is that Isaac Mayo took leave in order to build his estate in Maryland; another possibility is that Perry used his connections, which were considerable, to gain better assignments. Perry married into the Slidell family, wealthy and influential New York City merchants. His brother-in-law became a Democratic U.S. Senator at a time when Democrats were in power for long periods. Commodore Oliver Hazard Perry of Lake Erie fame was Matthew's brother, and his father had been a Captain in the U.S. Navy. Perhaps, of the greatest importance, Perry's sister had married Commodore Rodgers' younger brother, making the Commodore his brother-in-law. Rodgers was one of the highest ranking officers in the U.S. Navy.[2]

Isaac Mayo gained honor and respect for his service during the War of 1812. He had the good fortune to have participated in two of the famous single-ship actions of the war; the *Hornet-Peacock* in 1813 and the *Hornet-Penguin* in 1815; he received his training from two of the heroes of that war, James Lawrence and James Biddle. During the *Peacock* action, Midshipman Mayo received severe burns to his legs from a gun explosion. After the war he received a silver medal from the Congress and a dress sword from the State of Maryland, commemorating his service in those battles.[3]

Perry's service during the War of 1812 was unremarkable. He was aboard *President* for three cruises during which they captured prizes and fired their guns at vastly inferior British ships. He served on the *United States* and *President* while they were blockaded in port by the British. When the *President* did escape New York City in 1815 only to surrender to the British after a severe battle, Perry was not aboard--he was on his honeymoon leave. Thus, there was no combat glory for Perry during the war.

Perry became a Lieutenant in July, 1813; Mayo was elevated to that rank in February, 1815.[4] During the period of 1820 to 1824 Mayo struggled to get assignments. He served short periods as 1st Lieutenant (second in command) in *Ohio*, *Dolphin* and *Franklin*. Meanwhile, Perry spurted ahead in his career, serving as 1st Lieutenant in *Chippawa* and *Cyane*, then Commanding Officer of *Shark*. *Shark* was in Liberia for a time, and then in the West India Squadron fighting pirates. These two officers then served together on the *USS North Carolina* in 1826 and 1827. The *North Carolina* was new and the pride of the fleet; thus it was a prime assignment for both Perry and Mayo. Both had the rank of Lieutenant, but Perry was senior by about 1 1/2 years. Perry was assigned as the

First Lieutenant of the *North Carolina*, the flagship of Commodore Rodgers, the most senior officer in the Navy. Just prior to Mayo reporting to *North Carolina*, Perry became the acting Commanding Officer of the ship and remained in that position for the rest of their time aboard. Perry was promoted to Master Commandant on March 21, 1826. During his tour aboard *North Carolina*, Mayo received permission to take leave for a tour of Europe. He was gone from his post for a period of about five months, coming aboard just in time to return to the United States with the ship.[5] It appears that Mayo and Perry became good friends and respected each other during this service together, because when Perry was assigned as Commodore later in their careers, he usually chose Mayo to be the Commanding Officer of his flagship.

After leaving the *North Carolina* Mayo went on a 2 1/2 year leave. He was unmarried and there is very little information about his activities during that leave. Concurrently, Perry was assigned to Boston Navy Yard, where he acquired nice quarters for his family. He had an important job and an active social life. In April, 1830, he received command of the *USS Concord*, a new sloop-of-war, in which he then made a tour to the Mediterranean. Contrast Perry's duty with that for Mayo at the same time: Mayo received command of the *USS Grampus* in the West Indies. It was old and in terrible condition. Duty in the West Indies was considered to be atrocious because of the health conditions.[6] One begins to discern a trend here; Perry was receiving prime assignments, while Mayo was left with the dregs. No doubt both officers were meritorious--trained in the Rodgers system of strict discipline, and loyal to the Navy; Matthew Perry, however, had yet to face serious combat. Perhaps Perry's relationships, both his own Navy bloodlines, and his wife's connections, played an important part in his career advancement. Mayo was finally promoted to Master Commandant in April, 1832. By then he was about 6 years junior to Perry at this point in his career, which is difficult to explain on the basis of merit alone.

That pattern seems to recur increasingly as their respective career paths diverge. Perry requests and receives assignment to New York City in command of the recruiting station. He is promoted to Captain in 1837, and becomes Commandant of the New York Navy Yard in 1841, a Commodore's position. He remains there until his assignment as Commodore of the Africa Squadron in 1843. Meanwhile, Mayo takes almost six years of leave, during which time he marries and establishes his estate at Gresham in Anne Arundel County. His marriage to the daughter of the Chancellor of Maryland and former envoy to Brazil, is a stable and happy union. He received many financial benefits from his marriage and possibly a little leverage with the Maryland delegation in the U. S. Congress. Mayo commands the *USS Fairfield* on the Brazil Station for a year in 1837-1838 and the *Poinsett* during the Second Seminole War in Florida for about a year in 1839-1840. Both were hard sea duty, and the Florida duty was particularly unpleasant and hazardous. Mayo was promoted to Captain in September, 1841, still junior to Matthew Perry by four years. Perry, during this period, participated in modernization of the Navy, particularly the transition to steam propulsion. He pursued interests in recruiting, training, better opportunities for younger officers as well as modernization.[7] Perry wrote articles on these subjects, but his influence seems limited. Mayo's position on such subjects and his participation in advancing them remains unknown.

Thereafter, a new pattern emerges in the relationship between the two Navy Captains. Perry, assigned as Commodore of the Africa Squadron in 1843, requests that Mayo serve as the Commanding Officer of his flagship, the *USS Macedonian*. Mayo and Perry had served together on the *North Carolina* and agreed on how to run a ship. Mayo, now battle-tested, still strong and healthy, would be a good choice for a Commodore with considerable shore duty in his background. Later, Mayo is again seriously injured by a gun explosion (in his face when fighting with an African tribal chief who was intent on shooting Perry). Mayo killed the chief with his pistol bayonet, and no one else was injured. The injury was such that Mayo was returned home after just six months on the station; again, he had proven to be brave and effective when faced with unexpected circumstances.[8]

When the Mexican War started in 1846, both naval officers longed to be part of the first major war of their careers as senior officers. Perry was assigned as Vice Commodore to Commodore Conners, whom the Secretary of the Navy was trying to ease out. Perry was given command of the *USS Mississippi* at the same time. Interestingly, Perry's appointment came at the same time that President Polk sent Perry's brother-in-law to Mexico City with an offer to settle all controversies between the two nations. Possibly the brother-in-law suggested Perry for the position?

During the fall of 1846 Perry led three expeditions: Tabasco, Tampico, and Carmen in Yucatan. Several Mexican boats and ships were taken without gunfire, and mostly the cities surrendered without resistance, except at Tabasco during the first Tabasco expedition. At Tabasco there was gunfire on both sides, and two Americans were killed. Perry served as Vice Commodore until he had to return with his ship to Norfolk because of serious boiler problems. After completing boiler repairs in Norfolk, the *Mississippi* returned to Mexico, arriving off Veracruz on March 20, 1847. Mayo was the Commanding

Officer and Perry was the Commodore. Perry immediately relieved Commodore Conners and resumed support of the landings by the Army at Veracruz.

Once more Mayo "delivers" for Commodore Perry. The first day three American ships went aground in a severe storm. The *Mississippi* got underway and Mayo volunteered with four officers and a few seamen to take the barge to the ships to rescue the crew. They made three trips and rescued all of them. The Navy then landed guns and crews to assist the Army in the siege of Veracruz. Gunboats under Captain Tattnall were sent in close to bombard. Perry tried to withdraw them when Mexican gunners were shooting at close range at the gunboats, but Tattnall pretended not to see the signal. Mayo was sent in the barge through heavy enemy fire to tell Tattnall personally to withdraw. Then the naval guns began their bombardment. Mayo was ashore in charge of the bombardment when the wall was breached and the Mexicans stopped firing. He stood on the parapet and cheered with his gun crews, then rode off on horseback to tell the General and Commodore at their command post on the beach of the success. Much later General Scott remarked that Mayo was the bravest man he had ever known.

With Mayo installed as Governor of Alvarado, a captured Mexican town, Perry captured Tuxpan, a very fine victory. Next, on June 16, 1847, Perry landed an amphibious assault on Tabasco with Mayo as his Adjutant General. After great exertions marching and dragging guns along the route from their landing spot to the town, the battle did not involve much action. Once again, Perry was disappointed in not being able to lead hand-to-hand combat. No further naval actions occurred in Mexico; Mayo returned home for personal business after four active months.[9]

Mayo remained on leave until September, 1852, when he was ordered as Commodore of the Africa Squadron on the flagship *Constitution*. Perry remained in Mexico until June, 1848, and then had shore duty as General Superintendent of Mail Steamers until 1852. Back in his hometown of Tarrytown, New York, Perry's daughter had married August Belmont, an extremely wealthy New Yorker, who was an "ardent and generous supporter of the Democratic party." Perry later departed on his famous voyage to open Japan on November, 1852. Mayo desperately wanted to join Perry on this trip. From his Africa Squadron station he proposed to the Secretary of the Navy that he join Perry in *Constitution* as Vice Commodore. He argued that "her name alone would be a powerful reinforcement to any squadron of our Navy." He was needed in Africa, however, and was not ordered to leave.[10]

The similarity of the two officers' careers is striking; yet Perry always seemed to have the better job and the greater opportunities for achieving greatness. Mayo had a very fine career and was a solid naval officer, yet he never had the opportunity to achieve anything of historic proportions. Perry perhaps would have been in the same status, except for his final mission to Japan, a role that placed him in the history books. It appears that Mayo took opportunities to build up his estate in Maryland, but was not as attentive to his military career as he could have been, whereas Perry almost wholly devoted himself to his naval career. Whether these circumstances were by choice or chance, it cannot be determined.

There is some indirect evidence that Mayo chose the path that he took. He decided to take five months of leave from the *North Carolina* to tour Europe in 1826 and 1827; this could have been an important time for him, serving under Commodore Rodgers. Several times he cut short his Navy assignments in order to return home to attend to personal business. Such military assignments were expected to be two to three years. Mayo served only about one year in *Grampus* in the West Indies in 1830-1831 before requesting relief; he served about one year on the *Fairfield* on the Brazil Station in 1837-1838 before he was given permission to return home; he was assigned to the *Poinsett* in Florida in 1839-1840 for about 6 months before detachment; he served in the *Macedonian* on the African Station for about 10 months in 1843 before returning to the U.S., probably due to injuries; he spent only four months on the *Mississippi* in Mexico in 1847 before returning for personal business; and when he was Commodore of the Africa Squadron from 1852 to 1855, he kept up a steady stream of letters to the Secretary of the Navy to cut short the tour to two years. These circumstances couldn't have endeared him to his seniors in the Navy; certainly, in the aggregate these "shortened" tours of duty would not seem conducive to career advancement.

The appeal of Matthew Perry to historians is partly due to the extensive manuscript material available on both his life and military career. John H. Schroeder in his book on Perry published in 2000 lists sources such as several volumes of Perry personal letter books in the National Archives, the Rodgers Family Papers at the Historical Society of Pennsylvania and Perry papers at Harvard and Yale universities. In contrast, the Isaac Mayo papers are limited to two small journals and one letter book; his career has to be traced by the ships he served in and his Commodores. Matthew Perry benefits from a combination of source material and historical interest. The more known (and available) are the facts of Perry's life and career, the more enticement there is for historians to "weigh-in" on these sources, and so on, *ad infinitum.*

Mayo was the officer with the combat experience;

Perry was the officer with extensive shore duty, family influence and almost no battle experience. Perry earned his place in history with a non-combat role; more of a role as a diplomat than a naval officer. A side-by-side comparison of Mayo and Perry leads one to wonder whether either Perry's fame as a naval hero or Mayo's obscurity is warranted.

A
Chronology

19 Sept. 1791 (possibly later see Chapter 1)	Born at his father's home, Collersly, Anne Arundel County, Maryland.
15 Nov. 1809	Warranted a Midshipman.[1]
9 Jan. 1810	Appointed Midshipman.
12 Feb. 1810	Ordered to *USS Wasp*. Lt .James Lawrence, Commanding. Enforcing intercourse laws on coast.
3 July 1810	Entire crew transferred to *USS Argus* with James Lawrence. Enforcing intercourse laws along coast.
16 Nov. 1811	Ordered to *USS Hornet* with James Lawrence as commanding officer. Carrying messages to England and France.

21 June- Aug.1812	Sailed in *Hornet* on cruise in 31 Commodore Rodgers fleet. *Hornet* captured 3 ships.
6 Jan. 1813	Appointed prizemaster of schooner *Ellen* captured by *Hornet*.
14 Feb. 1813	Hornet defeats the British *Peacock*. Mayo injured with burns on legs.
1813-1815	Volunteered for the *Argus* to give battle to the *L.Cervier* in Long Island Sound. Volunteered under Decatur for defense of Washington. Sailed in *Hornet*--nearly captured by English Squadron. Volunteered under Biddle to meet English on Conn. River.
4 Feb. 1815	Commissioned Lieutenant.
23 March 1815	*Hornet*, under command of Biddle, defeats British ship, *Penguin*.
27 April 1815	*Hornet* escapes British line-of-battle warship, *Cornwallis*.

1815- 9 June 1820	Served as 1st Lt. in *Hornet* after 1817.
9 June 1820- 9 Aug. 1821	1st Lt. in *Ohio*, 74 guns.
9 Aug. 1821- 15 May 1822	1st Lt. in *Dolphin*, Pacific Squadron. Boarded a suspicious vessel alone. Had a severe conflict with her crew and drove them below.
15 May 1822- 18 Jan. 1823	1st Lt. in *Franklin*, 74 guns. In Pacific Squadron.
18 Jan.- 23 April 1823	Detached from *Franklin* in Valparaiso with dispatches. Traveled by way of Peru, Colombia, Panama and Mexico to reach U.S.
23 April 1823- 23 June 1824	First leave after 13 years of sea service.
23 June 1824- Nov. 1825	Recruited crew for *North Carolina*, testified in Commo. Stewart's trial and enroute to *North Carolina* on *Brandywine*.
Nov. 1825- 15 Aug. 1827	Served as Flag Lt. to Commodore Rodgers in *North Carolina* in Medit.

15 Oct. 1826- March 1827	Took leave and traveled in Spain, France, Switzerland and Italy for five months.
15 Aug 1827- 13 Feb. 1830	On leave.
13 Feb. 1830- 20 April 1831	Proceeded to West Indies and commanded the *USS Grampus.*
20 April 1831- 24 Feb. 1837	On leave.
20 Dec. 1832	Commissioned Master Commandant.
23 Sept. 1833	Married Sarah B.F. Bland.
24 Feb. 1837	Ordered to command of *USS Fairfield*, Brazil Station.
8 March 1838	Detached from *Fairfield* and returned home.
5 April 1839	Ordered to command force consisting of *Poinsett*, schooner *Wave* and barges to cooperate with Army against Florida Seminoles.

3 March 1840	Detached from command of *Poinsett*.
3 March 1840- 2 March 1843	On leave except for short special duty of 2 months.
8 Sept. 1841	Commissioned Captain.
2 March 1843	Ordered to command *USS Macedonian*, flagship of Commodore Perry in Africa Squadron.
13 Dec. 1843	Injured in fight with King Krako whom he killed. Exchanged commands to *USS Decatur* and returned to U.S.
9 Jan. 1845	Relieved of command of *USS Decatur*.
23 May 1845	Ordered to Examining and Advisory Board. Recommended location of U. S. Naval Academy to Annapolis.
9 Jan. 1845- 3 March 1847	On leave except for two short tours on Examining Boards.

3 March 1847- 10 July 1847	Commanded *USS Mississippi*, flagship of Commodore Perry in Mexico. Commanded Navy shore battery at Veracruz. Governor of Alvarado and Adjutant General of landing force at Tabasco.
10 July 1847- 16 Sept. 1852	On leave except for four short tours on Examining Board.
15 Sept. 1852- 2 June 1855	Commodore of Africa Squadron on *USS Constitution*. Captured American schooner, *H.N. Gambrill*.
2 June 1855- 1 May 1861	On leave except for one tour as Pres., Examining Board.
1 May 1861	Tendered his resignation.
18 May 1861	President Lincoln did not accept resignation and dismissed Mayo. Isaac Mayo dies.
26 May 1861	Congress confirmed Mayo's dismissal.

19 July 1977	Board for Correction of Naval Records recommended to Secretary of the Navy that Mayo's record be changed from dismissal to resignation accepted.[2] No action by the Secretary of the Navy was taken.
23 July 1980	Asst. Secretary of the Navy returned record to BCNR asking them to reconsider.
3 Oct. 1980	BCNR recommends Mayo's record be corrected based on the conclusion that he did not receive notice of the action of the President prior to his death.
18 February 1983	Asst. Secretary of Navy disapproved BCNR recommendation saying that they had not proven that he was not notified.
3 March 1995	BCNR again recommends a change in Mayo's record on the same basis as in 1980. The case was reopened as part of a review of all cases.

11 April 1997   Asst. Secretary of the Navy
                                 again disapproves the BCNR
                                 recommendation for the same
                                 reason given in 1983.

                                 .

                                 .

B
The Mayo Family

Abbreviations:

AA-Anne Arundel County, MD.

AH-All Hallows Parish records, Anne Arundel County, MD
　　　Number after AH indicates page.

bef.-before; b.-born; ca.-circa; d.-died; f.-page

MacIntire-*Annapolis Maryland Families*

MHM-Maryland Historical Magazine

All references are in the Maryland State Archives. Letter
　　　designations in wills, etc. indicate the book location.

Superscripts indicate generation after Joshua.

　　　The first of Commodore Mayo's ancestors in Anne Arundel County, MD, was his great-grandfather, Joshua Mayo. He first appeared in records when he married in 1707. The family is presented as descendants of Joshua.

Descendants of Joshua Mayo
Generation No. 1

　　　JOSHUA[1] MAYO died October 26, 1721, in Anne Arundel Cty., MD. He married HANNAH LEARSON July 10, 1707, in All Hallows Parish, MD. She died October 2, 1725, in Anne Arundel Cty., MD. (AH-101).

Notes for JOSHUA MAYO:
Joshua Mayo immigrated from Wales, according to Isaac Mayo's journal of 1826-1830.

Joshua Mayo was a witness on three deeds dated Sept. 7, 1710, in which Amos Garrett, merchant AA Cty., was the Grantee.

Joshua Mayo, AA Cty., recorded his cattle mark as a swallow fork in each ear on August 16, 1712, in LR, page 509. Joshua Mayo's marriage to Hannah Learson on July 10, 1707, is recorded in the All Hallows Parish records (AH-76).

Children of JOSHUA MAYO and HANNAH LEARSON are:

    i.   JOSEPH^2 MAYO, 1ST, b. May 8, 1708, All Hallows Parish, MD (AH-81 & 96).

    ii.   MARY MAYO, 1ST, b. February 10, 1709/10. (AH-96); d. August 5, 1711 (AH-96).

    iii.   JOSHUA MAYO, 2ND, b. July 4, 1715 (AH-96); d. October 11, 1716 (AH-86).

    iv.   JANE MAYO, b. September 4, 1717 (AH-96); d. October 2, 1725 (AH-101).

    v.   ELIZABETH MAYO, b. Dec. 6, 1719 (AH-96).

Generation No. 2

1. JOSEPH^2 MAYO, 1ST (JOSHUA^1) was born May 8, 1708, in All Hallows Parish, MD (AH-81 & 96). He married (1) SARAH STOCKETT July 10, 1735, in All Hallows Parish, MD (AH-119). He married (2) HENRIETTA MASSEY ca. 1754.

Notes for JOSEPH MAYO, 1ST:
Joseph Mayo was listed in the 1776 census with a family consisting
of 3 white males over 16, 3 white females, 5 white children, 8 black
males, 5 black women, and 7 black children. Joseph Mayo's inventory after his death was valued at $702 and included 10 slaves, 5
horses, 20 hogs, 12 sheep, 12 cattle, valuable furniture and china.
The inventory was done by Mary and Thomas Mayo and signed on
Sept 18, 1788, by Hannah, his executrix. Joseph Mayo's will (TG1,
f309) in 1786 was quite long and involved. He indicated that he
had already given land to his two sons, Thomas and Joseph (2nd),
from his first marriage. He gave to his son Joshua the plantation on
which Joseph (1st) lived. He gave to his son, John, all his lands in
Herring Creek. His son, Isaac, Sr., was to receive Colliersly (150
acres) and Brewers Chance Upheld (145 1/2 acres). He willed Selby's
Marsh which he bought from John Gresham in 1765, parts of which
were in dispute, to be divided equally between his two sons, James
and Samuel, once the dispute was settled. If Samuel died before he
was 21, his portion of land was to go to Isaac, Sr. This provision
would explain why Samuel left Selby's Marsh to Isaac, Jr. in 1801.

Children of JOSEPH MAYO and SARAH STOCKETT are:
  i.   JOSEPH[3] MAYO, 2ND, b. July 9, 1738, Anne
          Arundel Cty., MD.(AH-122); d. Anne Arundel Cty.,
          MD.

          Notes for JOSEPH MAYO, 2ND:
          Joseph Mayo signed Oath of Allegiance to MD in
          1777. On that list there were also Joseph Mayo,
          Sr. and Joseph Mayo, Jr. indicating that there were
          three men at that time. Joseph Mayo, Jr. is the son

of Thomas Mayo according to the final account of
the will of Joseph Mayo. Joseph Mayo (presumed
to be the Senior) is listed in the will in the same
way as the sons and daughters of Joseph Mayo,
1788.

ii.   THOMAS MAYO, SR., b. October 25, 1737,
      All Hallows Parish, MD (AH-120); d. 1796,   Anne
      Arundel Cty. MD...
iii. MARY MAYO, 2ND, b. July 26, 1739, Anne
      Arundel Cty., MD. (AH-83,96); d. 1795, Anne
      Arundel Cty., MD..

Children of JOSEPH MAYO and HENRIETTA MASSEY are:

iv.   ISAAC[3] MAYO, SR., b. January 9, 1759, Anne
      Arundel Cty., MD.(AH-149); d. 1797, Anne
      Arundel Cty., MD.
v.   JOHN MAYO, 1ST, b. October 13, 1756, All
      Hallows Parish, MD (AH-149); d. April 9, 1789,
      All Hallows Parish, MD.

      Notes for JOHN MAYO, 1ST:
      Listed in Joseph's Final Account and stated to be a
      son (1788). Patented Mayo's Addition in 1786 in
      AA Co., listed in Rent Rolls as 22 acres. James
      Mayo was his executor. He left his livestock to
      James and the residue to the estate to Henrietta
      Mayo (JG1, f66). Also left land called Crutchboys
      Choice to Joseph Jennifor and land in Herring Creek
      to his sisters Margaret and Henrietta Mayo. The
      Herring Creek land was inherited from his father,
      Joseph Mayo, 1st, in the will TG1, f309 in 1786.

His estate inventory was valued at $254 and included 5 horses, 7 cattle, 12 hogs, 4 sheep, $20 cash, 1/4 part of a certificate of $100 and 1/3 part of a $100 bond. It was signed by Joseph and Thomas Linthicum. His executor, James Mayo (a brother), signed the inventory on July 11, 1790. Date of his death is from his will. (JG1, f66)

vi. ANN MAYO, b. March 14, 1755, All Hallows Parish, MD (AH-149); m. JOSEPH JENNIFOR; d. August 10, 1810, MHM, Vol. 27, Page 182.
Notes for JOSEPH JENNIFOR:
Listed in Joseph's Final Account. Received land called Crutchboys Choice from John Mayo, his wife's brother in will (JG1, f66)

vii. MARGARET MAYO, b. January 13, 1771, All Hallows Parish, MD (AH-149).

viii. JAMES MAYO, b. April 04, 1765, All Hallows Parish, MD (AH-149); d. 1804, Anne Arundel Cty., MD..

ix. SAMUEL MAYO, b. September 23, 1778, Anne Arundel Cty., MD. (AH-157}; d. December 23, 1801, Anne Arundel Cty., MD. (AH-166).

Notes for SAMUEL MAYO:
In 1800 census he was 16-26 years old with 7 slaves. Joseph Mayo, 1st, his father, gave Selby's Marsh, Selby's Stop and Fortune to Samuel when he reached his 21st birthday. (TG1, f309) in 1786. If he should die before that time, the land was to go

to Isaac Mayo, Sr. It is probably for that reason that Samuel left the land to Isaac, Jr. when he died in 1801. In Federal Direct Tax roles of 1798 he was listed as having one dwelling house, one story, 30' x 16', 3 out houses, valued at $250. This house was probably Gresham.

In Samuel Mayo's will, JG2, f200, (Dec 8, 1801) he gave to Isaac, Jr. his land which he said he inherited from his father, Joseph. He stated that his mother was Henrietta and that Isaac Mayo, Sr. was his older brother. He also stated that Isaac, Jr. was the oldest son of Isaac, Sr. and that Joseph Mayo (3rd) was the son of Isaac, Sr. He stated that Sarah Mayo was his step-sister. She was the daughter of Joseph Mayo and Sarah Stockett. The land that he left to Isaac, Jr. was Selby's Marsh, Selby's Stop and Fortune with the proviso that when he was 21, he gave up his right to part of his father's (Isaac, Sr,) land to his younger brother, Joseph (3rd).

x.   HENRY MAYO, b. August 14, 1753, All Hallows Parish, MD. (AH-149).

Notes for HENRY MAYO:
Listed in the 1790 census as having 2 males below 16, 3 females, 6 other free whites and 15 slaves.

xi.   EDWARD MAYO, b. September 07, 1760, All Hallows Parish, MD. (AH-149).

xii. HANNAH MAYO, b. July 24, 1762, All Hallows
      Parish, MD. (AH-149).

xiii. HENRIETTA MAYO, b. July 17, 1768, All
      Hallows Parish, MD. (AH-149).

xiv. JOSHUA MAYO, 3RD, b. Bef. 1755, Anne
      Arundel Cty., MD.; d. June 01, 1812, Anne Arundel
      Cty., MD.

Notes for JOSHUA MAYO, 3RD:
Joshua Mayo, 3rd was an executor of the will of
his father, Joseph Mayo, 1st. (TG1, f309) in 1786.
The 1798 Federal Direct Tax showed him to have
a dwelling house 36' x 36', a kitchen 24' x 16', a
brick meat house 16' x 10', a corn house 24' x 10',
a granary 16' x 10' and 5 additional out houses.
All were valued at $500. He was listed in the 1800
census as over 45 years old and living alone. His
will left his lands, not listed, to two Stockett men,
suggesting that he may be the son of Joseph Mayo
and Sarah Stockett. His date of death is from his
will. His date of birth is from the 1800 census.
Joshua Mayo was listed in the Rent Rolls as
owning Dutchman's Point in 1766 and Town Hall
Enlarged in 1791.

2. MARY² MAYO, 1ST (JOSHUA¹) was born February 10, 1709/
10. She married PETER JOHNSON November 30, 1731, in All
Hallows Parish, MD.

Child of MARY MAYO and PETER JOHNSON is:
      i. HANNAH³ JOHNSON, b. December 8, 1732.

3. ELIZABETH² MAYO (JOSHUA¹) was born December 6, 1719, in All Hallows Parish, MD. She married JOHN RIDGLEY November 1, 1736, in All Hallows Parish, MD. (AH-120).
Children of ELIZABETH MAYO and JOHN RIDGLEY are:
> i. JOHN³ RIDGLEY, JR., b. September 13, 1739, All Hallows Parish, MD. (AH-121).
> ii. JOSHUA RIDGLEY, b. March 23, 1742/43, All Hallows Parish, MD.
>
> Notes for JOSHUA RIDGLEY:
> Birth date of Joshua Ridgely is from MacIntire, page 584.

Generation No. 3

1. THOMAS³ MAYO, SR. (JOSEPH², JOSHUA¹) was born October 25, 1737, in All Hallows Parish, MD (AH-120), and died 1796 in Anne Arundel Cty., MD. He married MARY -------. She died in 1795 in Anne Arundel Cty., MD.

Notes for THOMAS MAYO, SR.:
On Anne Arundel Cty Rent Rolls for 1760, 1766, 1769.
Had four land patents 1763-1776 (Bole Almanack Neck, 1763, Neglect or Rainy Day, 1766; Lucky Hole Enlarged, 1770; Major Potapsco Plain, 1776; all in AA Cty.) Information from Rent Rolls. Listed as a 2nd Lt. in August 2, 1776, from AA Cty in J. Boones Company of Maryland Militia (Archives of MD 11-141). This is the third ranking officer in a horse troop. See The Maryland Militia in the Rev. War by Clement and Wright. Commissioned Coroner of

Anne Arundel County, August 7, 1773. MHM Vol 27, Page 35.
Listed in the 1790 census as living alone with 5 slaves.

Notes for MARY -------:

Mary Mayo willed her silver watch to her son, Thomas, and 155
pounds to her son, Philemon, when he reached 21 years of age. The
155 pounds was the full amount left by his father, Thomas, for
Philemon. She also left to Philemon a piece of land called Town
Neck, purchased from John Morikin, containing 24 acres (JG1,
f485).

Children of THOMAS MAYO and MARY ------- are:

> i. THOMAS⁴ MAYO, JR., b. November 28, 1766,
> Anne Arundel Cty., MD.; d. January 3, 1798, Anne
> Arundel Cty., MD.; m. ANNE EVANS, June 13,
> 1790, Anne Arundel Cty. MD; b. October 3, 1762,
> All Hallows Parish, MD; d. October 3, 1828, Anne
> Arundel Cty., MD.
>
> Notes for THOMAS MAYO, JR.:
>
> Marriage date in *List of MD Marriages 1778-1790*,
> Robert Barnes. His will indicated that he had no
> children. He left to his wife the following land: the
> land north of Swan Creek or gut, part of Brandon
> (100 acres); Locust Thicket, 198 acres; and Lucky
> Hole Enlarged (102 acres). He willed his lands to
> the south of Swan Creek to his brother, Philemon
> Mayo, one part willed to him by his father and the
> other part by his brother, Joseph, Jr. He willed to
> Jacob Waters lands he owned in Montgomery Cty.
> William and John (157 acres), L---t (50 acres), and
> Friend in Need (70 acres) which he had purchased

from Jacob and Elizabeth Waters for 200 pounds. (JG2, f 21). His brother, Joseph Mayo, Jr., leaves him half of United Friendship and Point Lookout after Joseph's wife Hannah died. (THH2, f31) (1786-1787).

Notes for ANNE EVANS:
A tombstone for Ann Evans (Ann Soper) was found in 1998 in the Brockington subdivision off of Fort Smallwood Road in the northeastern part of Anne Arundel County, now called Solley Park. Audrey M. Bagley, Anne Arundel Readings, Vol 3, No. 1, January, 2000.

ii.   JOSEPH MAYO, JR., b. February 12, 1759, Anne Arundel Cty., MD.; d. December 7, 1786, Anne Arundel Cty., MD.; m. HANNAH -------.

Notes for JOSEPH MAYO, JR.:
Joseph Mayo, Jr. was listed in the Oath of Allegiance List of 1777 for males 18 years or older along with Joseph Mayo and Joseph Mayo, Sr. The final account of Joseph Mayo's will stated that Joseph, Jr. was the son of Thomas Mayo. The Archives of Maryland, 48-188, list Joseph Mayo, Jr. as an Ensign in the Maryland Militia beginning in Oct. 18, 1782. An Ensign was the junior officer in a troop of infantry. See *The Maryland Militia in the Rev. War* by Clement and Wright, 1987. Joseph Mayo, Jr. was listed in the 1776 census as having in his household: 1 white female, 5 white children and 1 black male. Birth and death dates are from MacIntire, page 458. His will (THH 2,

f31) did not indicate that he had children, but did state his wife's name was Hannah and his brothers were Thomas and Philemon. He willed Bole Almanack, Neglect or Rainey Day with the vacant land now called Point Lookout, 150 acres of United Friendship lying contiguous to Point Lookout to Hannah during her life. He gave to his brother, Philemon, the remainder of United Friendship. Point Lookout and Hannah's part of United Friend ship were to go to Thomas and Philemon after his wife's death.

iii.   PHILEMON MAYO, b. ca. 1780.

Notes for PHILEMON MAYO:
He received land south of Swan Creek owned by his brother Thomas Mayo, Jr who had inherited it from his father, Thomas, Sr., and his brother, Joseph, Jr. (JG2, f21). He was mentioned in his mother's, Mary Mayo, will to receive 155 pounds that his father, Thomas, Sr., had left him (JG1, f485). His brother, Joseph Mayo, Jr., mentioned him in his will to receive land from Joseph's wife, Hannah after her death. The land was a portion of United Friendship and Point Lookout. A portion of United Friendship was to go to Philemon directly (THH2, f31). This was in 1786-87.

iv.   SARAH MAYO, b. July 1, 1762, Anne Arundel Cty., MD.; d. November 25, 1814, Anne Arundel Cty., MD.

Notes for SARAH MAYO:
Data on Sarah Mayo from MacIntire, page 458
and her will made in 1814 (JG3, f71). She
apparently lived with Henrietta Norris, who was
the daughter of Joseph Mayo, 1st by his second
wife, Henrietta.

v. MORDECAI MAYO, b. December 15, 1764, Anne
Arundel Cty., MD.
Notes for MORDECAI MAYO:
Data on Mordecai Mayo is from MacIntire, page
458.

vi. MARY MAYO, 3RD, b. July 25, 1772, Anne
Arundel Cty., MD.

Notes for MARY MAYO, 3RD:
Data on Mary Mayo, 3rd from MacIntire, page
458.

2. MARY[3] MAYO, 2ND (JOSEPH[2], JOSHUA[1]) was born July
26, 1739, in Anne Arundel Cty., MD. (AH-83,96), and died 1795 in
Anne Arundel Cty., MD. She married FRANCIS LINTHICUM
January 28, 1755, in All Hallows Parish, MD. (AH-140). He was
born 1734 in Anne Arundel Cty., MD.

Notes for FRANCIS LINTHICUM:
Francis Linthicum owned Haslings (200 acres), Margarets Fields
(280 acres), and 25 acres of Turkey Point. These properties were
all in the Linthicum family since 1701. .

Children of MARY MAYO and FRANCIS LINTHICUM are:

    i.   JOSEPH4 LINTHICUM, b. October 19, 1757, All
           Hallows Parish, MD. (AH-140).

    ii. ELEANOR LINTHICUM, b. June 24, 1761, All
           Hallows Parish, MD. (AH-141).

   iii. THOMAS LINTHICUM, b. July 23, 1763, All
           Hallows Parish, MD. (AH-142).

   iv. SARAH LINTHICUM, b. September 4, 1765, All
           Hallows Parish, MD. (AH-143).

    v. RICHARD LINTHICUM, b. October 8, 1767, All
           Hallows Parish, MD. (AH-143).

3. ISAAC³ MAYO, SR. (JOSEPH², JOSHUA¹) was born January 9, 1759, in Anne Arundel Cty., MD.(AH-149), and died in 1797 in Anne Arundel Cty., MD. He married SARAH ANNE THORNTON before 1790, daughter of WILLIAM THORNTON and SARAH THORNTON.

Notes for ISAAC MAYO, SR.:
Isaac Mayo, Sr. signed an Oath of Allegiance to MD. in 1777. He had to be eighteen or older to sign. Isaac Mayo, Sr. along with his brothers, Joshua and John, was the executor of the will of Joseph Mayo, their father, in 1786. The three received a third of the estate and the rest of the children split a remaining third. Isaac, Sr. received Collersly and Brewer's Chance with all improvements. He also was to receive Selby's Marsh, Selby's Stopp and Fortune if his brother Samuel did not live until he was 21 years old. His brother did live and willed that land to Isaac, Jr. Sarah Ann Mayo was the executrix of his will. She remarried Jonathan Waters. She received 1/2 of Isaac's land during her widowhood, He left to his son, Isaac Mayo, Jr., the piece of land called Collersly containing his house with 150 acres. He left Brewer's Chance, 150 acres, to his son,

Joseph Mayo (3rd). His daughter received a Negro called Solomon. His personal property was to be divided with 1/3 to his wife and 2/3 to his daughter, Sarah, and son, George. The land, Brewer's Chance, was to be leased out until Joseph came of age and the proceeds divided between Isaac and Joseph when they became of age. (JG1, f 605). Sarah Ann Mayo, Isaac's wife, elected to receive 1/3 of his real and personal estate rather than the bequests in his will.. Isaac Mayo was listed in the 1790 census as having two females and 6 slaves. The inventory of Isaac's estate was valued at $422 and included 1 Negro man, 2 horses, 9 cattle, 26 sheep, 16 hogs, and gold and silver bank notes amounting to $99. The inventory was done by his sisters, Ann Jennifor and Margaret Lee. It was signed by his widow, Sarah Ann Mayo, on May 31, 1797.

Notes for SARAH ANNE THORNTON:
Sarah Ann Thornton Mayo married Jonathan Waters on Feb 17, 1798, after the death of her husband, Isaac Mayo, Sr. Wedding is recorded in All Hallows Parish according to Robert Barnes' book, Maryland Marriages. On Feb 5, 1823, she sold her right of dower (from the death of Isaac Mayo, Sr.) to Joseph Mayo for $100 for tracts of land in AA Cty. called Brewers Chance Upheld and Collersly. Thus, these were probably the properties on which Isaac Mayo, Jr. was born. The deed said Joseph Mayo already owned the property (WSG9, f213).

Children of ISAAC MAYO and SARAH THORNTON are:
      i.   HENRY⁴ MAYO, 2ND.
     ii.   JOHN MAYO, 2ND.

iii. ISAAC MAYO, JR., b. September 19, 1791, Anne
Arundel Cty., MD.; d. May 18, 1861, Anne Arundel
Cty., MD.

iv. EDWARD MAYO, 2ND.

v. SARAH HENRIETTA MAYO (1ST), b. ca. 1789,
Anne Arundel Cty., MD.; d. January 8, 1861,
Annapolis, MD; m. (1) ELIAS DORSEY; b. June
7, 1796; d. March 7, 1872, Bunker Hill, IL.; m.
(2) JAMES WILLIAMSON, September 26, 1809,
Annapolis, MD.; d. October 25, 1832, Annapolis,
MD.

Notes for SARAH HENRIETTA MAYO (1ST):
Marriage date, location and husband's name are
from book by Robert Barnes, Marriages, 1727-
1839. Date of death from MacIntire, page 771. This
marriage was second for James
Williamson.(MacIntire). On June 2, 1798, Jonathan
Waters was appointed the guardian of Sarah,
(Orphan's Court 4802, f28) He was the 2nd hus
band to her mother after her father, Isaac Mayo,
Sr., died.

Notes for JAMES WILLIAMSON:
Date of death from Maryland Gazette. James owned
Williamson Hotel in Annapolis along with his
partner, Thomas Swann. They also owned the mail
route from Baltimore and Washington to
Annapolis. James was a delegate to the State
Legislature from Annapolis. He appointed Isaac
Mayo one of his executors. Isaac was the brother

to James Williamson's wife (Chancery records 17898-11338A).

    vi.   GEORGE MAYO.

    Notes for GEORGE MAYO:
George was mentioned as receiving a portion of his father's property in the settlement of Isaac, Sr.'s will (JG1, f83) in 1798.

    vii.   JOSEPH MAYO, 3RD.

    Notes for JOSEPH MAYO, 3RD:
Joseph Mayo, (3rd) was willed Brewer's Chance Upheld by his father Isaac, Sr. The other parcel Collersly was left to Isaac, Jr. when he came of age. However, Isaac chose to receive Selby's Marsh, willed to him by Samuel Mayo, and gave up his right to Collersly to his brother, Joseph. Joseph purchased his mother's right of dower for $100 (WSG9, f213) in 1823 on both pieces. Joseph (3rd) was adopted by Jonathan Waters, his mother's second husband, June 16, 1798 (Orphan Court 4802, f28). He was receiving income from his father's estate which was paid to Jonathan Waters for room and board..

4. MARGARET[3] MAYO (*JOSEPH[2], JOSHUA[1]*) was born January 13, 1771, in All Hallows Parish, MD. (AH-149). She married EDWARD LEE ca. 1788.

Notes for MARGARET MAYO:
Margaret Mayo is listed as an heir in 1788 final account of Joseph
Mayo's Last Will and Testament.
Margaret Mayo received the land in Herring Creek belonging to
her brother, John Mayo, to be shared with her sister, Henrietta
(JG1, f 66).

Notes for EDWARD LEE:
Listed in Joseph's Final Account.

Child of MARGARET MAYO and EDWARD LEE is:
      i.   JOSEPH EDWARD[4] LEE, b. June 19, 1799, All
           Hallows Parish, MD. (AH-164).

5. JAMES[3] MAYO (*JOSEPH[2], JOSHUA[1]*) was born April 4, 1765,
in All Hallows Parish, MD. (AH-149), and died in 1804 in Anne
Arundel Cty., MD.

Notes for JAMES MAYO:
See JG2, f102 and JG2, f142.
James Mayo was listed in the 1790 census as having 2 males above
16, 1 male less than 16, 1 female and 5 slaves. There was a second
James Mayo listed in the 1790 census who has not been identified.
His brother, John Mayo,1st, made him the executor of his will and
left him farm animals. (JG1, f66) His father, Joseph Mayo, 1st, in
his will (TG1, f309) left part of his land described as part of Selby's
Marsh as follows: "begin the division line at the north end of the
NW by N line being the first line of the whole tract and running
thence across the said tract to the head of the easternmost branch of
the cove called the Spring Cove where the main Road down the
neck melded with the shore. All that part of Selby's Marsh lying on

the southeast side of the division and on the northeast and east of the aforesaid road to belong to my son, James."

Children of JAMES MAYO are:
    i.   WILLIAM⁴ MAYO.
    ii.   HANNAH MAYO, 2ND, m. JOHN WELLS, October 25, 1810, West River, MD.

        Notes for HANNAH MAYO, 2ND:
        Marriage date and husband are in book by Robert Barnes, *Marriages 1727-1839*.

    iii. JOHN MAYO, 3RD.

6. HENRIETTA³ MAYO (*JOSEPH², JOSHUA¹*) was born July 17, 1768, in All Hallows Parish, MD. (AH-149). She married THOMAS NORRIS.

Notes for HENRIETTA MAYO:
Henrietta Mayo received from her brother, John Mayo, 1/2 the land he owned in Herring Creek. (JG1, f66)

Children of HENRIETTA MAYO and THOMAS NORRIS are:
    i.   MARY⁴ NORRIS.

        Notes for MARY NORRIS:
        Received 100 pounds, furniture, and personal effects from Sarah Mayo in her will of July 30, 1814.

    ii. JOHN NORRIS.

Generation No. 4

1. ISAAC⁴ MAYO, JR. (*ISAAC³, JOSEPH², JOSHUA¹*) was born September 19, 1791, in Anne Arundel Cty., MD., and died May 18, 1861, in Anne Arundel Cty., MD. He married SARAH BATTAILE FITZHUGH BLAND September 23, 1833, daughter of THEODORIC BLAND and SARAH DAVIES. She was born 1808, and died November 23, 1885.

Notes for ISAAC MAYO, JR.:
The birth date of Isaac Mayo is in question. The monument in the Naval Academy cemetery indicates he was born in 1795; however his obituary states he was born Sept. 19, 1791. The 1860 census also would place Isaac's birth in 1791 The evidence in the wills of his nephew, Samuel Mayo, and his father, Isaac Mayo, Sr., would indicate that the earlier date of 1791 is more accurate. Samuel states that Isaac was the oldest son of Isaac, Sr. in his will written in 1801. Isaac, Sr. said that he had four children: Isaac, Jr., Joseph, Sarah and George in his will written in 1797. The 1790 census indicated that Isaac, Sr. was married with one female child (possibly Sarah). Thus it is known that Joseph and George were younger than Isaac, Jr. and that George was a baby. Two eighteen month intervals between children from 1797 would place Isaac in 1793-1794. It is not known how many children were born and died during that period. On June 16, 1798, Isaac, Jr. was adopted by Jonathan Waters. He was receiving income from his father's estate and later from his Uncle Samuel's estate. This money was paid to Jonathan Waters for room and board until he entered the Navy in 1809.

Notes for SARAH BATTAILE FITZHUGH BLAND:
Birth and death dates are from MacIntire, page 458.

Children of ISAAC MAYO and SARAH BLAND are:

i. THEODORIC[5] MAYO, b. 1841, Anne Arundel Cty., MD.; d. September 26, 1843. Buried in St. Anne's Cemetery, Annapolis ..

Notes for THEODORIC MAYO:
Birth and death date from MacIntire, page 458.

ii. WILLIAM JOHNS MAYO, b. August 18, 1846, Anne Arundel Cty., MD.; d. October 1, 1875, Anne Arundel Cty., MD.

Notes for WILLIAM JOHNS MAYO:
Birth and death dates from MacIntire, page 458.

iii. SOPHIA BLAND MAYO, b. September 19, 1839, Anne Arundel Cty., MD. (AH-177); d. December 28, 1915, Baltimore, MD.

iv. SARAH HENRIETTA MAYO (2ND), b. June 24, 1836, Anne Arundel Cty., MD. (AH-176); d. September 01, 1842, Anne Arundel Cty., MD.

Notes for SARAH HENRIETTA MAYO (2ND):
Death date is from MacIntire, page 458.

Generation No. 5

1. SOPHIA BLAND⁵ MAYO (*ISAAC⁴, ISAAC³, JOSEPH², JOSHUA¹*) was born September 19, 1839, in Anne Arundel Cty., MD. (AH-177), and died December 28, 1915, in Baltimore, MD. She married THOMAS H. GAITHER September 29, 1857, in Ellicott City, MD, son of GEORGE GAITHER and HANNAH BRADLEY. He was born October 15, 1835, in Baltimore, MD., and died September 23, 1918, in Catonsville, MD.

Notes for SOPHIA BLAND MAYO:
All data from MacIntire, page 258.

Notes for THOMAS H. GAITHER:
All data from MacIntire, page 258.

Children of SOPHIA MAYO and THOMAS GAITHER are:
  i.   THOMAS H. GAITHER⁶ ,JR.
  ii.   GEORGIANA MAYO GAITHER,d. November 1945, Baltimore, MD.

Generation No. 6

1. GEORGIANA MAYO⁶ GAITHER (*SOPHIA BLAND⁵ MAYO, ISAAC⁴, ISAAC³, JOSEPH², JOSHUA¹*) died November, 1945, in Baltimore, MD. She married JAMES LAWRENCE BAILLIERE November 9, 1893, in Howard County, MD. He was born December 23, 1865, in Orange, N.J., and died February 20, 1917, in MD.

Notes for JAMES LAWRENCE BAILLIERE:
Owned Peggy Stewart House in Annapolis, MD. All data from
MacIntire, page 26.

Children of GEORGIANA GAITHER and JAMES BAILLIERE
are:

    i.   THOMAS HENRY GAITHER[7] BAILLIERE, b.
          June 18, 1897; d. March 30, 1973, Baltimore, MD.

    ii.   LAWRENCE MAYO BAILLIERE, b. November
          25, 1899; d. October 21, 1964, Ft. Lauderdale, FL.

          Notes for LAWRENCE MAYO BAILLIERE:
          USNA non-graduate, Class of 1922. All data from
          MacIntire, page 26. Buried in Mayo plot, St. Anne's
          Cemetery, Annapolis, MD.

Generation No. 7

1. THOMAS HENRY GAITHER[7] BAILLIERE (*GEORGIANA
MAYO[6] GAITHER, SOPHIA BLAND[5] MAYO, ISAAC[4], ISAAC[3],
JOSEPH[2], JOSHUA[1]*) was born June 18, 1897, and died March 30,
1973, in Baltimore, MD.

Notes for THOMAS HENRY GAITHER BAILLIERE:
USNA non-graduate Class of 1919. All data from MacIntire, page
26.

Child of THOMAS HENRY GAITHER BAILLIERE is:

    i.   THOMAS HENRY GAITHER[8] BAILLIERE, JR.

C
Building an Estate

An important part of Commodore Mayo's personal life was the building of an estate. The sources of the money he used to acquire land cannot be definitely stated, but examination of the events in his life and the land acquisitions suggest several possibilities. By 1860 he had accumulated over 1400 acres of land in the Mayo area of Anne Arundel County, Maryland. He also owned land in Pensacola, Florida, and his wife owned her father's estate in Howard County.

He was proud of the land that he accumulated during his long career in the Navy and attributed his success in putting his estate together to "his forefathers and his own management." Commodore Mayo was the son of Isaac Mayo, Sr., a Revolutionary War veteran, who was not in good health because of his war experience. The father of Isaac Mayo, Sr. was Joseph Mayo, who had married twice, had 14 sons and daughters from both marriages and who was quite successful as a plantation owner. Joseph's land was located primarily in the area between the South and Rhode Rivers in Maryland, now called Mayo. When Joseph died in 1786, he willed the part of his land called Collersly and Brewers Chance to Isaac Mayo, Sr. and part of his land called Selby's Marsh, Selby's Stop and Fortune to his son, Samuel, if he lived to be twenty-one. If Samuel did not live, the land was to go to Isaac Mayo,

Sr.[1] Joseph had purchased Collersly (this is also spelled Colliersly after the original owner named Colliers) from Joseph Brewer and Samuel Geist on January 29, 1774, for 410 pounds.[2]

Isaac Mayo, Sr. was born in 1759, the second son of Joseph's second marriage, and married Sarah Anne Thornton before 1790 (he is listed in the 1790 census as having two females in his household, a wife and daughter presumably). Isaac, Jr., the future Commodore, was his oldest son. Isaac Mayo, Sr. died in 1797 willing Collersly to Isaac, Jr. and Brewer's Chance to his son, Joseph, when he reached 21 years of age.[3] Samuel Mayo, Isaac Mayo, Sr's brother, did live to be 21 years old, but died two years later in 1801. He had willed his land, Selby's Marsh, Selby's Stopp and Fortune to Isaac Mayo, Jr. when he reached 21 provided that he gave up his right to Collersly to Isaac Mayo, Jr.'s brother, Joseph.[4] When Isaac Mayo, Jr. turned 21 he chose to take Selby's Marsh (which contained the Gresham house), Selby's Stop and Fortune (about 250 acres). His brother, Joseph, then owned Collersly and Brewer's Chance (about 250 acres). Joseph purchased the right of dower from his mother for $100 in 1823.[5] The Federal Direct Tax Rolls of 1798 lists Samuel Mayo's home, probably Gresham, as one story, 30' by 16', with three out houses valued at $250. This 250 acres was the cornerstone of the Mayo estate.

After the death of Isaac Mayo, Jr.'s father in 1797, his mother remarried Jonathan Waters in 1798. Isaac would have been very young, and may not have known his father. The Jonathan Waters family lived in the same area. Church records show that two step-brothers, William Thornton Waters and Thomas Gassaway Waters, were born in the 1799 to 1801 years. Isaac apparently grew up with his step-father's family.

Jonathan Waters was appointed guardian to Sarah, Isaac and Joseph, the three surviving children of Isaac Mayo, Sr,, on June 16, 1800. He filed Guardian Account statements with the Orphan's Court each year. In the case of Isaac, the final account was in 1809, at which time Isaac became a Midshipman in the U.S. Navy.[6] The accounts show that Isaac by then was receiving income from both his father's and his Uncle Samuel's estates. Nearly all of the money was paid to his step-father for board and lodging each year, so that it is unlikely that he had much money from this source

Isaac Mayo's Navy record shows that he was attached to Navy ships continually from 1810 to August 31, 1827. He probably had short visits to the Annapolis area, but had little opportunity to manage his inheritance. One land record indicates that he borrowed money on his Selby's Marsh land and Gresham in March, 1820.[7] At that time he was still attached to the *Hornet*. He borrowed $8500, signing over the Selby Marsh land to William Brewer. The payment schedule permitted either James Williamson, his sister's husband, or Mayo to make the payments. Mayo had received money from three prizes awarded the crew and officers of the *Hornet*; Congressional awards for the capture of the British ships *Peacock* and *Penguin* and money from the capture of the British merchant ship *Ellen*. These were probably considerable sums of money, but it seems unlikely that he would have mortgaged his land, had he still had money from those awards. Isaac was not assigned to any Navy duty for 2 1/2 years from August 31, 1827, to March 1, 1830; however, there is no record of any activity in improving his land holdings during that interim.

In 1832 Isaac Mayo was promoted to Master Commandant and started almost six years of inactivity in the Navy. In February, 1833, he received a clear title to the Selby's Marsh land and home, Gresham,[8] as a result of paying off the mortgage. At about the same time he was appointed executor of his brother-in-law's estate, James Williamson who died quite wealthy, owning the Williamson Hotel in Annapolis in partnership with Thomas Swann. Possibly the Williamson estate paid the Selby Marsh mortgage. On September 23, 1833, Isaac married Sarah Battaile Fitzhugh Bland, daughter of Theodoric Bland and Sarah Davies. Theodoric Bland was quite wealthy and prominent, serving as the Chancellor of Maryland. Isaac Mayo was able to purchase additional land on January 15, 1835, when he bought Cotter's Desire (256 acres) for $2927.50.[9] Cotter's Desire was adjacent to and south of Selby's Marsh. The timing of the purchase would suggest that the money used may have come from his wife or his father-in-law.

Mayo next added 37 acres of land in the old Turkey Point Road area on the eastern border of Cotter's Desire, purchasing it from Thomas Brashears for a sum of $740.[10] This purchase was made on January 2, 1842, shortly after Mayo's promotion to Captain on September 8, 1841. He had requested that he be relieved from duty in the Brazil Squadron an April 30, 1838, to attend to his sister's estate. He was actually relieved on August 30, 1838, so that possibly some money was being received from that source during this time period.

Captain Mayo was ordered to command of the *Macedonian* on March 2, 1843. The ship was deployed to Africa to suppress the slave trade. Towards the end of December, 1843, Mayo traded commands with the Commanding Officer of the *Decatur* and returned to the United States. He remained attached to that ship until January 9, 1845. On June 10, 1843, Mayo purchased Little Island, about 42 acres, and Ramsay Gut, about 136 acres (now called Ramsay Lake) from the Estate of John Whittington.[11] The timing of this purchase was probably related to its availability in an estate. In 1845 and 1846, Captain Mayo served on the examining boards for midshipmen and was primarily at home. He added to his land holdings by purchase of the land called Big Island, Linthicum Island or Haslings (now called Turkey Point). He paid $1800 for the approximately 167 acres from the Estate of Thomas Daniel Lee on August 14, 1845.[12]

From March to July, 1847, he served as Commanding Officer of the *Mississippi* off the coast of Mexico during the Mexican War. He commanded the Naval Battery during the bombardment of Veracruz, was Adjutant of the landing forces in the attack on Tabasco and later was Governor of Alvarado for a short time.

Mayo requested that he return to the U. S. apparently because his father-in-law, Theodoric Bland, had died in November, 1846, naming Isaac Mayo as his executor. Theodoric's will was somewhat complicated.[13] He had made provisions for his wife and son William and left the rest to Isaac's wife and their children. William Bland was not able to care for his affairs because of a horseback accident, and Isaac was later appointed his guardian. William's holdings were to go to Isaac's wife and children after his death. During these years Isaac Mayo purchased two more small pieces of land from the Estate of Thomas Daniel Lee, one in November, 1847, and the other in May, 1848.[14] These pieces of land are described as being at the junction of the south side of the South River and the Chesapeake Bay and probably were adjacent to the Turkey Point land that he bought in 1845. In 1848, 1849 and 1850 he served on the examining board for Midshipman and thus again was home most of the time. Commodore Mayo had his land surveyed by John Duvall on October 14, 1852, and it was patented by Anne Arundel County January 3, 1854, as Gresham. The survey plat showed that he owned about 1000 acres by then. That plat can be found in the Maryland State Archives; it is the source of much of the information shown on the table and map at the end of this chapter.

One can assess and summarize Gresham and its lifestyle by the 1850's. Mayo owned few slaves, just 6 men and 3 women above the age of 21; there were 13 additional children.[15] Apparently, the slaves were used mainly for house work and transportation. Mayo's holdings were farmed by tenant farmers: the land was quite productive. In one of his personal letters he mentions taking his managers and tenants to the voting poll place in his carriages, confirming that his farming was done by tenants. The agricultural assessment in 1850 shows that he had 1000 acres of land, 750 acres of which was farmed. It was evaluated as worth $20,000 plus improvements of $400. He had 14 horses, 7 milk cows, 15 cattle, 58 sheep and 84 swine with a combined value of $1300. On average he produced 2500 bushels of wheat, 5000 bushels of corn, 500 bushels of oats, 25,000 lbs. of tobacco, 175 lbs. of wool, 50 lbs. of Irish potatoes and 300 lbs. of butter each year. In a personal letter written while he was aboard the *Constitution* he comments that "he possesses ample wealth, entertains and moves about like a Gentleman and presents gifts to his friends." Overall, the information available indicates that by 1850 Isaac Mayo was a wealthy and prominent man in Maryland, as he continued to buy land around Gresham. It is probable that income from his plantation and the U. S. Navy was adequate by this time to purchase additional land.

Mayo was assigned as Commodore of the African Squadron aboard the *USS Constitution* on September 6, 1852, which sailed from New York on March 2, 1853, and returned from Africa on June 2, 1855. He wrote in a letter to the Secretary of the Navy in 1854 that a close relative of his wife's had died and left an estate to his wife. This probably would have been her disabled brother, William Bland. After his return he continued to accumulate land to the west of his Gresham estate. He purchased 178 acres from the William Sanders Estate on November 16, 1855; 39 acres from William Dawson on April 4, 1856; and another 200 acres from the Soleman Gafford Estate in November, 1856.[16] He then owned 1429 acres of the Mayo peninsula. Possibly, money from the estate of William Bland helped pay for the additional land.

The table, "Sources of Commodore Mayo's Land," includes the titles, dates, deed identification, and the current name of the land. The map, "Commodore Mayo's Land in 1860," shows the approximate location of each of the pieces of land that he acquired. Not all of the land could be cultivated; some was marsh and 129 acres were in Ramsay Lake.

Isaac Mayo wrote his will on December 26, 1860,[17] and died about five months later. He decided to divide his land into two parts, one part to go to the children of his daughter, Sophy (then married to Thomas Gaither), and the other part to go to his son, William (then 14 years old), when he reached 21 years of age. The land north of a line he described as running from White Marsh Creek to a gate on the road and then dividing Lake Ramsay (he called it Lake Bland) in half would go to William. This was the old part of the Mayo land, including Selby's Marsh, Cotters Desire, Little Island and Turkey Point (which he called Mayo Island) and consisting of 776 acres. The land to the south of the line going to Sophy's children was all the newer land that he had purchased in the 1840s and 1850s and consisted of 700 acres.

William did live to inherit the land, but he did not marry and died in 1875 when he was only 29 years old. Thus, all of the land eventually went to the two children of Thomas and Sophy

Gaither, Thomas H. Gaither, Jr. and Georgiana. Eventually all of the land was sold to various buyers and developed into residential communities.

Sources of Commodore Mayo's Land

Title	Acres	Previous Owner	Date	Deed	Current Name
Part of Selby's Marsh	253	Samuel Mayo	1812-1816	Will-JG2,200	River Club Estates
Part of Fortune	43	Samuel Mayo	1812-1816	Will-JG2,200	Holly Hill Harbor
Part of Cotter's Desire	244	Thomas Cowman Estate	1-13-1835	WSG19,401	Ponder Cove
Between Cotter's Desire and Little Island	37	Thomas Brashears	1-2-1842	WSG26,82	Old Turkey Point
Little Island and Ramsay Gut	29	John Whittington Estate	6-10-1843	WSG26,633	Little Island and Ramsay Lake
	129				
Part of Hasling	101	Thomas Lee Estate	8-14-1845	JHN1,254	Turkey Point
			10-13-1847	JHN3,65	
			5-6-1848	JHN3,270	
Part of Margaret's Field	92	William Bland	7-1847	I. Mayo is appt.Trustee	Shoreham Beach
Linthicum Stopp	84	William Sanders Estate	10-29-1852	NHG1,513	Part Harbor View
Total in 1852	**1012**				
Part of Pleasant Prospect	178	William Sanders Estate	11-16-1855	NHG5,104	West Shore
		(See note 18)			
	39	William Dawson	4-4-1856	NHG5,384	Mayo Beach
Part of Hastings	200	Soleman Gafford Estate	11-16-1856	NHG6,51	Harbor View
		(See note 19)			
Total in 1856	**1429**				

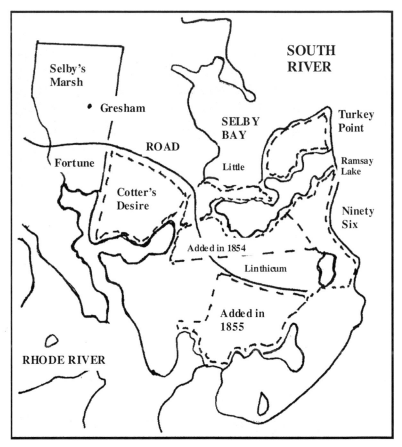

MAYO LAND HOLDINGS IN 1860

D
Mayo Artifacts

Artifacts from Commodore Mayo's military career and his personal life are relatively rare, considering how prominent and well-known he was during his lifetime. Listed below are those that have been identified during the preparation of this book.

Gresham. This is one of the most important artifacts from Isaac Mayo's lifetime. It has been restored and is located on Mayo Road in Edgewater, MD. A photograph of Gresham is included in Chapter 1. There are inconsistent dates for the age of the original part of this house. The owners have understood that it was first built in 1686. The book, *Anne Arundel's Legacy*, contains the following about Gresham, "The central core is marked by two large brick fireplaces and incorporates evidence of the original late eighteenth century one-and-a-half story hall-and-parlor plan dwelling. Two two-story wings flanking the main block were added in the mid-nineteenth century."[1] The owner reports that the foundation is local stone; the main beams are oak and interior studs are black walnut. The house is a National Historic Place.

Several items formerly belonging to Isaac Mayo were auctioned on November 20, 1989, by Butterfield and Butterfield, Los Angeles, CA. All items were sold and now are in the hands of private owners. They are listed below as they were described in the catalog for the auction:

Important and Historic War of 1812 Gold Eagle Sword Presented to Lt. Isaac Mayo. The entire delicate hilt of solid gold. The grips fully chased in ornate relief designs of floral sprays, pole arms and banners, all bordering the bearded head of Neptune on both sides. Exquisite detailed eagle head pommel finely beaded at the base. Emblemized on the counter guard a raised American eagle and shield over a panoply of flags, cannon and battle trophies, the whole terminating in upswept finials of full eagle heads. The straight 27" blade marked "W. Rose" and etched in detailed segments depicting naval engagements of the U.S.S. Hornet. The obverse with three panels, the upper inscribed "Peacock and Hornet 1814" with details of both vessels, on the center section an American eagle and shield with "E. Pluribus Unum" riband. The lower captioned "Escape of the Hornet from the Cornwallis 1815" with etchings of both ships. The reverse center inscribed "Presented to Lieut. Isaac Mayo, March, 1828, as the Reward of Patriotism and Valor." Flanked on both ends, details of the ships Hornet and Penguin, and a cannon with stand of flags. The leather sheath mounted with solid gold bands, the top with high relief fouled anchor, flag trident and pike encircled by a laurel wreath. An allegory of Neptune, seated on a chariot drawn through the ocean by a pair of steeds, adorns the middle section. The tip decorated in oak leaves and scroll motifs. Condition: The hilt and scabbard mounts in mint condition. Blade slightly faded. The scabbard leather expertly replaced.

Extremely Rare Cased 2 1/2" Diameter Silver Medal Struck by an Act of Congress and Presented to Lieut. Mayo. Hand engraved on the outer case, "Navy Department Feb 10, 1820. Sir, in compliance with resolution of Congress of the U.S. the President directs me to present to you a silver medal in testament of the high sense entertained by Congress of your gallantry and good conduct and service in the capture of the British sloop of war, Penguin, after a brave and skillful combat...Smith Thompson." The front of the medal a bust of the Hornet's captain, and relief worded "The Congress U.S. to Lieut. Isaac Mayo for his Gallantry, Good conduct and Service." The reverse a relief design of the naval engagement between the two vessels and worded "Capture of the British ship Penguin by the U.S. ship, Hornet, off Tristan D'Acunha March XXIII, MDCCCXV" Listed in the book, "Medallic History of the U.S.," by Loubat.

Original 13" x 10" Pencil and Watercolor Drawing. Of the exact sword inscribed "Copied from the original sword by E.C. Young, and presented to Martin William John Mayo...ship Constitution, September, 1854." (Note: This was possibly Master William Johns Mayo, the young son of Isaac Mayo.)

Original 13" x 10" Pencil and Watercolor Drawing. Inscribed "A Battalion of Seamen and Marines from the U. S. Frigate Constitution at Drill and Target Practice on Whale Island Harbor of Porto Praya, Nine November 1854. By E.C. Young for Commo. Mayo."

Model 1852 U.S. Naval Officer's Sword and Scabbard. In near mint condition. The hilt retaining 100% gilt finish, mint sharkskin grips. The 30" blade marked "Ames, Chicopee, Mass."

Leather scabbard excellent to mint, with all gilt finish, and engraved on the top mount "Commodore Isaac Mayo, U.S. Navy"

Pieces of Early 19th century Silver Flatware. Struck with maker's hallmarks and engraved with either the name "Mayo" or the monogrammed letter "M."

Miscellaneous other Mayo items are listed below:
A Mexican War Cannon. Obtained during the Mexican War and brought back by Mayo. The cannon is located at Gresham. Inscriptions are included in Chapter 9.

A Mexican War Cannon Ball. Also obtained during the Mexican War by Mayo. It is 13" in diameter and stamped "San Juan de Ullo."

Mexican War Cannons at the U.S. Naval Academy. There are many cannons on the grounds of the Naval Academy that are marked Mexican War or attributed to Commodore Perry from the Mexican War. Mayo was partly responsible for gathering and transporting these pieces.

Two Marble Column Bases and an Iron Urn on a Square of Marble. Mayo found these during his tour of duty on the *USS North Carolina* in the late 1820s. They came from the Island of Delos, near Greece. All are located at Gresham. See Chapter 3.

The Sternboard of the *USS Macedonian*. This was the ship that Mayo commanded in Africa The sternboard is located in Dahlgren Hall, U. S. Naval Academy, on the north side, inside, above the entrance. See Chapter 8.

A Scrapbook. Probably kept by Isaac Mayo's wife. It is located at the Maryland Historical Society. The scrapbook was sold with the contents of Commodore Mayo's library to the father of Mrs. Mary McGuire, New York City. She returned it to the Maryland Historical Society.

A Portrait of Isaac Mayo. Attributed to Benjamin West, 1838. Owned by the State of Maryland and now in storage. Maryland Commission on Artistic Property of the Maryland State Archives, MSA SC 1545-1196. A copy of this portrait is included in the front material of this book.

A Second Portrait of Isaac Mayo. This portrait is identical with the portrait owned by the State of Maryland. Owned by Mr. Tom Bailliere, a descendant of Isaac Mayo. Both portraits appear to be originals.

Two Private Journals and a Letter Book. "Private Journal of Isaac Mayo, Esq., Commodore Commanding U. S. Forces on the West Coast of Africa", "Private Letters from 1809 to 1830, I Mayo" and "Private Journal at Sea from 1826 to 1830, I. Mayo, USN" are at the Navy Museum Library, Washington, D.C. and were purchased from Parke-Barnet Galleries, Madison Ave., New York City in 1968.

Sea Chests. One is about 18" high and wide and 36" long. Probably pine wood and stenciled on front with "The Star Spangled Banner, Long May It Wave, O'er Land of the Free and the Home of the Brave." A stencil, in color, of a patriotic crest. is also included. Believed to be owned by Isaac Mayo; now owned by Mr. Tom Bailliere, a descendant of Isaac Mayo.

A second sea chest is located in the South River Club house, marked with the name of Captain Isaac Mayo.

Eagle Emblem from the Sternboard of the *USS Hornet.* Donated to the Maryland Historical Trust by the Bailliere family and now displayed at the Maryland Historical Museum in Baltimore, Md.

Portrait of Elias Glenn. Dated 1803 and formerly the property of Theodoric Bland, the father of Isaac Mayo's wife. Inherited by Isaac Mayo after Theodoric Bland's death. Theodoric Bland married Sarah Glenn, but it is uncertain exactly how Elias Glenn was related to Sarah. The date of 1803 on the Elias Glenn portrait would be consistent with a relationship of brother to Sarah Glenn Bland. According to Isaac Mayo's journal, Sarah Glenn was born in Londonderry, Ireland, and immigrated with her father, William Glenn. The portrait is now owned by Mr. Tom Bailliere.

Catalog of Antique Fragments. There is a list of these fragments collected by Isaac Mayo during 1826 and 1827 in Greece and other areas of Europe. The items are numbered from 1 through 47. Items are identified with descriptions such as, "From Plains of Old Troy." The catalog is contained in his Private Journal from 1826 to 1830 now in the Navy Museum Library, Washington, D.C.

Notes

Illustrations

1. Courtesy Maryland Commission of Artistic Property of the
   Maryland State Archives MSA SC 1545-1196. An
   identical painting of Isaac Mayo is owned by Mr. Tom
   Bailliere, a Mayo descendant. The second painting is
   attributed to John W. Jarvis.

Preface

1. John H. Schroeder, *Matthew Calbraith Perry*, xi

Chapter 1: Isaac Mayo's Personal Life

1. AHP, 76. M221, MSA.
2. I. Mayo, USN, Private Journal at Sea from
    1826-1830,NMLW.
3. IM LTR to SN of Nov. 23, 1854. LTRs Received by
    SN from COs of Squadrons, M VB 255.1.S7, R107, 71,
    NAL.
4. AAC Wills, TG1, 309 (1786), MSA.
5. Ibid., JG1, 605 (1797), MSA
6. Ibid., JG2, 200 (1801), MSA
7. AHP, 163. M221, MSA.
8. AAC Testamentary Papers, JG2, 384 (1809), MSA.
9. IM Journal, 1826-1830, NMLW.
10. AAC Land Records, WSG7, 62 (1820), MSA.
11. AAC Chancery Papers, 17898-11338A (1833), MSA.
12. AAC Land Records, WSG17, 536 (1833), MSA.
13. Ibid., WSG19, 401 (1835), MSA.
14. AAC Wills, TTS1, 555 (1846). Chancery Papers,
    17898-9467 (1847), MSA.
15. All birth and death dates from Robert Henry McIntire,
    Annapolis, Maryland Families, 458.

16. IM LTR to SN of Oct 23, 1837. LTRs Received by SN from Commanders, M VB 255.1.M3, R21, 69, NAL.
17. AAC Chancery Papers, 17898-9467 (1847), MSA.
18. The Sun, Baltimore, May 24, 1861, MCALL.
19. Solomon H. Sanborn, *An Exposition of Official Tyranny in the United States Navy*, 6-7, NAL.
20. Mayo Scrapbook, 75, MHS..
21. Ibid., 50.
22. IM LTR to SN of Nov. 23, 1854. LTRs Received by SN from COs of Squadrons, M VB 255.1.S7, R107, 71, NAL.
23. IM LTR to Commodore, Bureau Navy Yards and Docks, (personal) of Nov 23, 1854. LTRs Received by SN from COs of Squadrons, M VB 255.1.S7, R107, 71, NAL.
24. AAC Wills, BEG1, 461 (1860), MSA.
25. The Sun, Baltimore, May 24, 1861, MCALL.
26. Mayo subject file, NMLW.
27. Naval Historical Foundation Publication, *Going South*, Series II, Number 27, Fall, 1981, Appendix, pages 34 and 35.
28. Mayo subject file, NMLW.
29. William Oliver Stevens, *Annapolis, Anne Arundel's Town*, 201.

Chapter 2: War of 1812

1. Military record is from enclosures to LTR to BCNR, Commodore Isaac Mayo, USN (Deceased) of 13 July 1977, G1264, MSA.
2. Albert Gleaves, *James Lawrence*, 73-79.
3. Ibid., 79-88.
4 Ibid., 91.

5. Ibid., 101, 105.

6. Ibid., 114, 123,

7. IM LTR to SN of Nov. 15, 1854, LTRs Received by SN from COs of Squadrons, M VB 255.1.S7, R107, 68, NAL.

8. Albert Gleaves, *James Lawrence*, 123.

9. Theodore Roosevelt, *The Naval War of 1812*, 165, 166.

10. Albert Gleaves, *James Lawrence*, 125, 126, 127, 137, and IM LTR to SN of Nov. 15, 1854, LTRs Received by SN from COs of Squadrons, M VB 255.1.S7, R107, 68, NAL.

11. Ibid., (Gleaves), App. 303, 304 and A. Bowen, *The Naval Monument*, 36-39.

12. Ibid., (Gleaves), 138, 140.

13. Theodore Roosevelt, *The Naval War of 1812*, 178-193.

14. David F. Long, *Sailor-Diplomat, A Biography of Commodore James Biddle*, 1783-1848, 47.

15 Ibid., 48.

16. IM LTR to SN of Nov. 15, 1854, LTRs Received by SN from COs of Squadrons, M VB 255.1.S7, R107, 68, NAL.

17. David F. Long, *Sailor-Diplomat, A Biography of Commodore James Biddle*, 50-52.

18. Theodore Roosevelt, *The War of 1812*, 431.

19. Ibid., 433-435.

20. A. Bowen, *The Naval Monument*, 187.

21. Maryland Historical Magazine, Vol. XII, No. 3, Sept. 1917, 230 and Vol. XX, 1925, 255.

22. Butterfield and Butterfield, "Historic American Swords," Auction Lot 6149, NAM.

23. IM LTR to SN of Nov. 15, 1854, LTRs Received by SN from COs of Squadrons, M VB 255.1.S7, R107, 68, NAL.

24. IM Private Letterbook for 1809-1830, NMLW.
25. IM LTR to SN of Dec. 20, 1836, LTRs Received by SN from Commanders, M VB 255.1.M3, R 21, 77, NAL.

Chapter 3: *USS North Carolina* in the
        Mediterranean, 1825-1827
1. Charles Oscar Paullin, *Commodore John Rodgers*, 339.
2. Samuel Eliot Morison, *"Old Bruin" Commodore Matthew Calbraith Perry*, 96, 97.
3. Ibid., 85.
4. Ibid., 86, 97.
5. Charles Oscar Paullin, *Commodore John Rodgers*, 327, 328.
6. Samuel Eliot Morison, *"Old Bruin" Commodore Matthew Calbraith Perry*, 90, 91.
7. Ibid., 97, 98.
8. Commodore Rodgers LTR to SN, July 18, 1826, Area Files of the Naval Record Collection, M VB 255.2.A7, Area 4, R5, 196, NAL.
9. Ibid.
10. Personal observation by the author.
11. Samuel Eliot Morison, *"Old Bruin" Commodore Matthew Calbraith Perry*, 98.
12. Ibid., 101, 102.
13. Ibid., 102.
14. Enclosures to LTR to BCNR, Commodore Isaac Mayo, USN (Deceased) of 13 July 1977, G 1264, MSA.
15. Maryland Historical Magazine, Vol XII, No. 3, Sept.1917, 230.

Chapter 4: Travel in Europe, 1826-1827
1. IM Private Journal, 1826-1830, NMLW.

Chapter 5: West India Squadron, 1830-1831

1. David F. Long, *Sailor-Diplomat, A Biography of Commodore James Biddle*, 100, 101.
2. Gardner W. Allen, *Our Navy and The West Indian Pirates*, 41, 54, 55.
3. Ibid., 51, 52.
4. Francis B. C. Bradlee, *Piracy in the West Indies and Its Suppression*, 22.
5. Gardner W. Allen, *Our Navy and The West Indian Pirates*, 85-89.
6. LTRs Received from Captains, January 29, 1831, M VB 255.1.C3, R153, 84, NAL
7. Ibid., April, 1830 to May, 1831, R145-157.
8. Ibid., May 3, 1830, R146, 47.
9. Ibid., June 1, 1830, enclosure to R146, 47.
10. IM Private Letter Book, (May 24, 1830), NMLW.
11. Ibid., (June 21, 1830).
12. LTRs Received from Captains,Sept. 11, 1830, R150, 49 and Nov. 1, 1830, R152, 13, M VB 255.1.C3, NAL.
13. Ibid., Jan. 18, 1831, R153, 69.
14. Ibid., March 22, 1831, R155. 79.
15. Ibid,, January 17, 1831, R153, 91.
16. Ibid., March 6, 1831, R155, 19 and April 19, 1831, R156, 110.
17. Ibid., July 24, 1831, R159, 8.

Chapter 6: Brazil Squadron, 1837-1838

1. IM LTR to SN, April 14, 1837, LTRs Received by SN from Commanders, M VB 255.1.M3, R21, 44, 89, 100, NAL.

2. Ibid., June 7, 1837, R21, 117.
3. Commodore Renshaw LTR to SN, July 8, 1837, LTRs Received by SN from Captains, M VB 255.1.C3, R229, 292, NAL.
4. LTR from LCDR Ogden, *USS Dolphin*, Aug. 1, 1837, LTRs Received by SN from Commanders, M VB 255.1.M3, R21, 27, NAL.
5. IM LTR to SN, Aug. 17, 1837, LTRs Received by SN from Commanders, M VB 255.1.M3, R21, 26, NAL.
   6. IM LTR to LCDR Purviance, *USS Dolphin*, Oct. 13, 1837, LTRs Received by SN from Commanders, M VB 255.1.M3, R21, 47, NAL.
7. IM LTR to SN, Oct. 23, 1837, LTRs Received by SN from Commanders, M VB 255.1.M3, R21, 69, NAL.
8. Commodore Nicholson LTR to SN, Nov. 20, 1837, LTRs Received by SN from Captains, M 255.1.C3, R233, 47.
9. Boris Fausto, *A Concise History of Brazil*, 54-92 and Roderick J. Barman, *Brazil, The Forging of a Nation, 1798-1852*, 195-198.
10. Commodore Nicholson LTR to President of Province of Bahia, Nov. 28, 1837. LTRs Received by SN from Captains, M 255.1.C3, R235, 10, NAL
11. LTRs from IM to U.S. Consul, Bahia and replies, Dec. 17-21, 1837. :LTRs Received by SN from Captains, M 255.1.C3, R 235, 18, NAL.
12. LTR from Legation of U.S. to Commodore Nicholson, Jan. 22, 1838, and reply of Jan. 31, 1838, LTRs Received by SN from Captains, M 255.1.C3, R236, 61, NAL.
13. LTR from Commodore Nicholson to IM, Jan. 14, 1838, LTRs Received by SN from Captains, M 255.1.C3, R235, 18, NAL.

14. LTR from Commodore Nicholson to U.S. Charge d'Affairs, Rio de Janeiro, Jan. 31, 1838, LTRs Received by SN from Captains, M 255.1.C3, R236, 61, NAL.
15. IM LTR to Commodore Nicholson, Feb. 6, 1838, LTRs Received by SN from Captains, M 255.1.C3, R236, 34, NAL.
16. LTR from Commodore Nicholson to SN, Feb. 24,1838, LTRs Received by SN from Captains, M 255.1.C3, R236, 61, 62, NAL.
17. Ibid., August 30, 1838, R 242, 458, NAL.

Chapter 7: Second Seminole War, 1839

1. IM LTR to SN, Nov. 15, 1854, LTRs Received by SN from COs of Squadrons, M VB 255.1.S7, R 107, 68, NAL.
2. George E. Buker, *Swamp Sailors, Riverine Warfare in the Everglade*, 14, 15.
3. Ibid., 14, 25, 26, 69-81.
4. Ibid., 84, 85.
5. LTR to BCNR, Commodore Isaac Mayo, USN (Deceased) of 13 July 1977, G1264, MSA.
6. SN to Shubrick, June 14, 1839, LTRs sent by the SN to Officers, M VB 255.1.U6, R29, NAL.
7. IM to SN, June 17, 1839, LTRs Received by SN from Commanders, M VB 255.1.M3, R23 and SN to IM, June 22, 1839, LTRs sent by the SN to Officers, M VB 255.1.U6, R29, NAL.
8. Charles B. Stuart, *Naval and Mail Steamers of the United States*, 32, 33.
9. IM to SN, Aug. 23, 1839, LTRs Received by SN from Commanders, M VB 255.1.M3, R23, NAL.

10. Ibid,, June 17, June 26, June 30, July 3, July 6, July 13, 1839.

11. George E. Buker, *Swamp Sailors, Riverine Warfare in the Everglades*, 86, 87.

12 IM to SN, July 25, and July 30, 1839, LTRs Received by SN from Commanders, M VB 255.1.M3, R23, NAL.

13. George E. Buker, *Swamp Sailors, Riverine Warfare in the Everglades*, 88.

14. IM to SN, Aug. 4, Aug 6, Aug 16, Aug. 23, Aug. 26, 1839, LTRs Received by SN from Commanders, M VB 255.1 M3, R23, NAL.

15. Ibid., Sept. 8, Sept. 17, 1839.

16. Ibid., Oct. 2, Oct. 13, Oct. 26, 1839.

17. Ibid., Oct. 13, Nov. 15, Nov. 30, 1839 and George E. Buker, *Swamp Sailors, Riverine Warfare in the Everglades*, 91.

18. Ibid., Dec. 27, 1839.

Chapter 8: Africa Squadron, 1843

1. James Coleman Pfautz, *The African Squadron of the United States Navy, 1843-1861*, Appendix A.

2. Ibid., Appendix B and Mayo Scrapbook, 25, MHS.

3. MHM, Vol. XII, No. 3, 210.

4. Samuel Eliot Morison, *"Old Bruin" Matthew Calbraith Perry*, 164-167.

5. James Coleman Phautz, *The African Squadron of the United States Navy*, 16, Appendix F.and Samuel Eliot Morison, *"Old Bruin" Commodore Matthew Calbraith Perry*, 168.

6. Ibid.(Phautz), 52 and ibid. (Morison), 169.

7. Samuel Eliot Morison, *"Old Bruin" Commodore Matthew Calbraith Perry*, 168.

8. Ibid., 166 and James Coleman Phautz, *The African Squadron of the Unites States Navy*, 24.
9. James Coleman Phautz, *The African Squadron of the United States Navy*, 35-37.
10. Samuel Eliot Morison, *"Old Bruin" Commodore Matthew Calbraith Perry*, 171 and Penelope Campbell, *Maryland in Africa*.
11. Ibid., (Morison), 172 and William Elliot Griffis, *Matthew Calbraith Perry*, 172.
12. Ibid., (Morison), 173 and (Griffis), 174.
13. Ibid., (Morison), 174.
14. Ibid., (Morison), 174 and (Griffis) 175-180.
15. Enclosures to LTR to BCNR, Commodore Isaac Mayo, USN (Deceased) of 13 July 1977, G1264, MSA.
16. Riley, Elihu S., *A History of Anne Arundel County in Maryland*, 88, 89.
17. Park Benjamin, *The United States Naval Academy*, 145.
18 Riley, Elihu, S., *The Ancient City*, 264, 265.
19. Crane, John and Kieley, Lt. James F., *The First Hundred Years*, 21, 27.

Chapter 9: Mexican War, 1847
1. Samuel Eliot Morison, *"Old Bruin" Commodore Matthew Calbraith Perry*, 206.
2. Ibid., 193.
3. Ibid., 194-206.
4. William Elliot Griffis, *Matthew Calbraith Perry*, 219, 220.
5. Ibid., 232, 233 and Samuel Eliot Morison, *"Old Bruin" Commodore Matthew Calbraith Perry*, 218.
6. Ibid. (Griffis), 234-236, (Morison), 219 and Mayo Scrapbook, 74, MHS.

7. Mayo Scrapbook, 50, MHS.
8. Samuel Eliot Morison, *"Old Bruin" Commodore Matthew Calbraith Perry*, 223, 224 and William Elliot Griffis, *Matthew Calbraith Perry*, 239, 240.
9. Ibid. (Morison), 233, 235, 237 and (Griffis), 243-250 and Charles Lee Lewis, *Admiral Franklin Buchanan*, 121.
10. Ibid. (Lewis), 122.
11. AAC Chancery Records, July 1847 Term, MSA.
12. Samuel Eliot Morison, *"Old Bruin" Commodore Matthew Calbraith Perry*, 178.
13. Mayo Scrapbook, 75, MHS.
14. Emily Taylor, "Discovering Our School Community," 10.

Chapter 10: Commodore in *USS Constitution*, 1852-1856

1. Sir Alan Moore, *Sailing Ships of War*, 37.
2. IM Private Journal, 1852-1856, NMLW.
3. Ibid., and IM LTRs to SN (Feb. 12 and 26, March 3, Aug. 20, 1853), LTRs Received by SN from COs of Squadrons, M VB 255.1.S7, R107, 5, 12, 13, 22, NAL.
4. Ibid., (May 15, 1853), 14.
5. Ibid., (June 13, 1853), 15.
6. Ibid., (July 17, 1853), 17.
7. Ibid., (July 18, 1853), 18.
8. IM Private Journal, 1852-1856, NMLW.
9. IM LTRs to SN (July 21, 1853), LTRs Received by SN from COs of Squadrons, M VB 255.1.S7, R107, 19, NAL.
10. Ibid., (Nov. 27, 1853), (Jan. 20, 1854), (April 3, 1854), 37, 41, 44.

11. Ibid., (Aug. 22, 1853), 23.
12. Ibid., (Sept. 14, 1853), 27.
13. Ibid., (Nov. 10, 1853), 36.
14. IM Private Journal, 1852-1856. NMLW.
15. IM LTRs to SN (March 10, 1854), LTRs Received by SN from COs of Squadrons, M VB 255.1.S7, R 107, 43, NAL.
16. Ibid., (Nov. 10, 1853), 36.
17. Ibid., (April 20, 1854), 46.
18. Ibid., (Nov. 23, 1854), 71.
19. Ibid., (April, 27, 1855), (May 23, 1855), 87,91.
20. Ibid., (June 2, 1855), 95.

Chapter 11: Assessment of Isaac Mayo's Career
1   Abstracts of Service Records of Naval Officers, 1778-1898, M330, NA.
2. Samuel Eliot Morison, *"Old Bruin" Commodore Matthew Calbraith Perry*, 53,54 and John H. Schroeder, *Matthew Calbraith Perry*, xix.
3   IM LTR to SN (Nov. 15, 1854), LTRs Received by SN from COs of Squadrons, M VB 255.1.S7, R107, 68, NAL; A. Bowen, *The Naval Monument*, 187; and Maryland Historical Magazine, Vol. XII, No. 3, Sept. 1917, 230.
4   Samuel Eliot Morison, *"Old Bruin" Commodore Matthew Calbraith Perry*, 39, 40, 41, 49, 50 and John H. Schroeder, *Matthew Calbraith Perry*, xix.
5. Ibid., (Morison) 97, (Schroeder), xix., IM LTR to SN (Nov. 15, 1854), LTRs Received by SN from COs of Squadrons, M VB 255.1.S7, R107, 68, NAL and IM Journal, 1826-1830.

6. Ibid., (Schroeder), xix. and IM LTR to SN (Nov. 15, 1854).
7. Ibid., (Schroeder), xix., IM LTR to SN (Nov. 15, 1854) and Robert Henry McIntire, *Annapolis, Maryland Families*, 61, 458.
8. Ibid., IM LTR to SN (Nov. 15, 1854).
9. Samuel Eliot Morison, *"Old Bruin, Commodore Matthew Calbraith Perry*, 194-206, 215-227.
10. Ibid., (Morison), 250, 253, 254, 289 and IM LTRs to SN (July 18, 1853), LTRs Received by SN from COs of Squadrons, M VB 255.1.S7, R107, 18.

Appendix A: Chronology.
1. Military record is from Statement of Services of Isaac Mayo, U. S. Navy, NA, enclosures to LTR to BCNR, Commodore Isaac Mayo, USN (Deceased) of 13 July 1977, G1264, MSA, and IM LTR to SN of Nov 15, 1854, LTRs
Received by SN from COs of Squadrons, M VB 255.1.S7. R 107, 68, NAL.
2. Isaac Mayo subject file, NMLW.

Appendix B: Building an Estate
1. AAC Wills, TG1, f309 (1786), MSA.
2. AAC LR, BEG1. f319 1774), MSA.
3. AAC Wills, JG1, f605 (1797), MSA.
4. Ibid., JG2, f200 (1801), MSA.
5. AAC LR, WSG9, f203 (1823), MSA.
6. AAC Testamentary Papers, JG2, f384 (1809), MSA.
7. AAC LR, WSG7, f62 (1820), MSA.
8. Ibid., WSG17, f536 (1833), MSA.
9. Ibid., WSG19, f401 (1835), MSA.

10. Ibid., WSG26, f82 (1842), MSA.
11. Ibid., WSG26, f633 (1843), MSA.
12. Ibid., JHN1, f254 (1845), MSA.
13. AAC Chancery Records, July 1847 Term, MSA.
14. AAC LR, JHN3, f65 (1847) and JHN3, f270 (1848), MSA.
15. Federal Census, Maryland, AAC, 1st District, Slaves, Sept. 14, 1850, MSA.
16. AAC LR, NHG5, f104 (1855); NHG5, f384 (1856) and NHG6, f51 (1856), MSA.
17. AAC Wills, BEG1, f461 (1860), MSA.
18. The 1852 survey of Gresham done by John Duvall shows 33 acres north of Little Island as foul and another 129 acres in Ramsay Gut is also shown covered with water. This is somewhat consistent with the 1850 Agricultural Census that shows Isaac Mayo having 775 acres as improved and 250 acres unimproved.
19. A description of the land purchased in November, 1856, was not found; however by a process of elimination, based on the land that Commodore Mayo owned at his death, it would be the land south of Ramsay Lake and north of the road.

Appendix D: Mayo Artifacts
1. Donna Ware, *Anne Arundel's Legacy*, 83.

Bibliography

UNPUBLISHED OFFICIAL RECORDS AND MANUSCRIPTS

All Hallows Church Records, microfilm, Maryland Hall of Records.

Anne Arundel County Chancery Records, microfilm, Maryland Hall of Records.

Anne Arundel County Land Records and Rent Rolls, microfilm, Maryland Hall of Records.

Anne Arundel County Testamentary Papers, microfilm, Maryland Hall of Records.

Anne Arundel County Wills, microfilm, Maryland Hall of Records.

Federal Agricultural Census, Maryland, Anne Arundel County, First District, 1850, microfilm, Maryland Hall of Records.

Federal Direct Tax Roles of 1798.

Isaac Mayo Private Journal, Commodore Commanding U.S. Forces on the West Coast of Africa, 1852-1856. Navy Museum Library, Washington, D.C.

Isaac Mayo Private Journal, 1826-1830. Navy Museum Library, Washington, D.C.

Isaac Mayo Private Letter Book, 1809-1830. Navy Museum Library, Washington, D.C.

Isaac Mayo subject file, Navy Museum Library, Washington, D.C.

Letter to the Board for Correction of Naval Records, 13
July 1977, "Commodore Isaac Mayo, USN" with
enclosures.

Map, Isaac Mayo Certificate of Gresham, 1851, Maryland
Hall of Records.

Mayo Scrapbook, Maryland Historical Society, MS 583.
Baltimore, MD.

Taylor, Mrs. Emily. "Discovering Our School Community,"
by Grade V, Mayo Elementary School, 1952-1953.

United States Census Report, Maryland, Anne Arundel
County, 1790, 1800, 1850 slaves, 1850, microfilm,
Maryland Hall of Records.

United States Department of the Navy Records, microfilm,
U.S. Naval Academy Nimitz Library and National
Archives
Letters Received by the Secretary of the Navy from
Captains, 1807-1861.
Letters Received by the Secretary of the Navy from
Commanders, 1804-1886.
Letters Received by the Secretary of the Navy from
Squadrons, 1841-1886.

United States Department of the Navy Records, National
Archives
Abstracts of Service Records of Naval Officers,
1798-1898
Statement of Services of Naval Officers to Dec. 31,
1841.
Letterbook of Naval Officer Resignations, Civil
War.

BOOKS AND ARTICLES

Allen, Gardner W. *Our Navy and The West Indian Pirates.* Essex Institute. Salem, Mass., 1929.

Bagley, Audrey M. "Anne Arundel Readings," Vol. 3, No.1, January, 2000.

Barman, Roderick J. *Brazil, The Forging of a Nation, 1798-1852.* Stanford University Press, 1988.

Barnes, Robert. *Marriages and Deaths from the Md. Gazette, 1727-1839.* Genealogical Pub. Balt. 1973.

Bowen, A. *The Naval Monument.* A. Bowen. Boston, 1816.

Bradlee, Francis B.C. *The Suppression of Piracy in the West Indies, 1820-1832.* Essex Institute. Salem, Mass., 1922.

Buker, George E. *Swamp Sailors, Riverine Warfare in the Everglades, 1835-1842.* The University Presses of Florida. Gainsville, 1975.

Butterfield and Butterfield. *Historic American Swords, November 20, 1989, Los Angeles.* Auction Lot Number 6149

Campbell, Penelope. *Maryland in Africa.* University of Illinois Press. Urbana, Chicago, London, 1971.

Clement and Wright. *The Maryland Militia in the Revolutionary War.* 1987.

Crane, John and Kieley, Lt. James F. *The First Hundred Years.* McGraw-Hill Book Co. New York, 1945.

Dearborn, H.A.S. *The Life of William Bainbridge, Esq. of the United States Navy.* Princeton University Press. Princeton, 1931.

Fausto, Boris. *A Concise History of Brazil.* Cambridge University Press. 1999.

Gleaves, Albert. *James Lawrence, Captain, United States Navy.* G. P Putnam's Sons. New York, 1904.

Griffis, William E. *Matthew Calbraith Perry: A Typical American Naval Officer*. Boston: Cupples and Hurd, 1887.

Hartzler, Daniel P. *Marylanders in the Confederacy*. Family Line Publications. Silver Springs, Md., 1986.

Lewis, Charles Lee. *Admiral Franklin Buchanan: Fearless Man of Action*. The Norman, Remington Co. Baltimore, 1929.

Long, David F. *Sailor-Diplomat: A Biography of Commodore James Biddle, 1783-1848*. Northeastern Universicty Press. Boston, 1983.

Loubat, J. F. *The Medallic History of the United States of America, 1776-1876*. Loubat. New York, 1878.

MacIntire, Robert Henry. *Annapolis, Maryland Families*. Baltimore, 1979.

Maclay, Edgar Stanton. *A History of the United States Navy*. D. Appleton Co. New York, 1898.

Maryland Historical Magazine, "Men of Maryland Specially Honored by the State or the United States," Vol. XII, Sept. 1917. No. 3; "Unpublished Letters from the Archives," Vol. XX , 1925; "The Linthicum Family and Branches," Vol. XXV, 1930. Maryland Historical Society.

Moore, Sir Alan. *Sailing Ships of the War, 1800-1860*. Halton & Truscott Smith Ltd., London. Minton, Balch & Co., New York, 1926.

Morison, Samuel Eliot. *"Old Bruin" Commodore Matthew C. Perry 1794-1858*. Little, Brown and Company. Boston, Toronto, 1967.

Mullins, Caroline L. Britt. *The History of Mayo, Maryland*. Gateway Press, Inc. Baltimore, Md., 1996.

Naval Historical Foundation Publication, Series II, Number 27, Fall 1981. "Going South: U. S. Navy

Officer Resignations and Dismissals on the Eve of the Civil War."

Obituary, Commodore Isaac Mayo and "Death of Com. Mayo". The Baltimore Sun, May 24, 1861.

Paullin, Charles Oscar. *Commodore John Rodgers*. The Arthur H. Clarke Co. Cleveland, Ohio, 1910.

Pfautz, James Coleman. *The African Squadron of the United States Navy, 1843-1861*. Masters Thesis, The American University, 1968.

Riley, Elihu S. *A History of Anne Arundel County in Maryland*. C.G. Feldmeyer. Annapolis, 1905.

Riley, Elihu Samuel. *"Ancient City" History of Annapolis in Maryland*. Record Printing Office. Annapolis, 1887.

Roosevelt, Theodore. *The Naval War of 1812*. Haskell House Publishers Ltd. New York, NY, 1882

Sanborn, Solomon, H. *An Exposition of Official Tyranny in the United States Navy*. New York, 1841.

Schroeder, John H. *Matthew Calbraith Perry, Antebellum Sailor and Diploma*t. Naval Institute Press. Annapolis, Md., 2001.

Stevens, William Oliver. *Annapolis: Anne Arundel's Town*. Dodd, Mead and Company. New York, 1917.

Stuart, Charles B. *Naval and Mail Steamers of the United States*. 1853.

Ware, Donna M. *Anne Arundel's Legacy*. Anne Arundel County. 1990.

Index

About the Author

Byron A. Lee is a retired U.S. Navy Captain and former naval engineer. He lives with his wife in southern Anne Arundel County about five miles south of the former home of Commodore Isaac Mayo. He is the author of one other book, *The Mercers and Parkhurst*, about the history of the local area and the home in which he lives.

Captain Lee is a graduate of the U.S. Naval Academy in the Class of 1950 and received his Master's Degree from the Massachusetts Institute of Technology. His military career was primarily in engineering; specializing in nuclear power plant design, construction and testing. Following his retirement from the Navy, he worked twenty years at a private engineering firm. He has always been interested in history; retirement has given him the opportunity to research, write and publish.

Patron List

Our thanks to the patrons, listed below, who contributed so generously to our pre-publication subscription request.

We are especially grateful to the exceptional generosity of **Thomas and Anne Bailliere, Jr.**, and **Owen and Marian Daly II**. Thomas Bailliere, Jr. and Marian Daly are direct descendants of Commodore Isaac Mayo.

Many of our patrons gave generously to the Jack Kelbaugh Memorial Publication Fund and we are honored to acknowledge these bequests. The ongoing support of **Stanley and Elizabeth Kelbaugh Westendorf** is particularly noteworthy in this regard.

In addition to the patrons listed above, we sincerely thank the following:

AMI of Anne Arundel County
Mr. and Mrs. Tyras S. Athey
Capt. Louise Bareford
Milton W. & Linda L. Barrett
Bertha C. Bonner
John & Joanne Boone
James B. & Mary M. Calvert
James W. Cheevers
Sharon L. Cook
Capt. David F. & Joan V. W. Cunningham
Isabel Shipley Cunningham

Mr. & Mrs. Robert M. Davis
Roy F. & Rosemary B. Dodd
Rose M. Ebbert
Mary Lou Egan
Eben D. Finney III
Sylvia G. Garrison
Charles W. & Nancy C. Gaston
Harry D. Greenwell
Dennis & Bonney Grote
John T. Gurney III
John H. & Mary Ruth Hammond
Col. & Mrs. Harry E. Hasslinger
Forrest G. & Mildred B. Hoffmaster
Charles & Inge Hofmeister
Dave and Pam Hovatter
Angelina C. Jones
Carolyn P. Keenen
The Jack Kelbaugh Family
Cathern S. Kline
Theodore J. Kreyling
Gustav S. & Bonnie K. Kurtz
Capt. & Mrs. John M. LeCato
O. James Lighthizer
James Douglas Linthicum
Robert Edward Linthicum
Alfred J. & Irene H. Lipin

William F. List
Barbara Lynch
John W. McCarley, Jr.
Mary-Joan McHugh
Barrett L. & Anne H. McKown
Mr. and Mrs. Ronald McMorrow
Jane W. McWilliams
Amy E. Mahanes
Eugene & Barbara Makowski
Ted & Ellen Mathison
L. Roy & Betty Norbeck
Clifford Michael Phelps
Clifford Rodger Phelps
Carroll T. & Hester B. Richardson
Jean B. Russo
Mark N. & Ann R. Schatz
Emma M. Schramm
Robert F. Smith
Sara Anne Stinchcomb
Elizabeth N. Sullivan
Judi R. Teplitz
Frank S. & Paula D. Tremel, Jr.
William T. & Lois H. Upton, Jr.
Richard & Elma Watson
Walton D. & Irene A. Wilson
John L. & Carolyn T. Wisthoff